Business Result

Skills for Business Studies

Intermediate

Louis Rogers

OXFORD
UNIVERSITY PRESS

Contents

3

1 Motivation

Study focus

1 What motivates you in life? Rank the following in order from most important (1) to least important (8). Does anything else motivate you?

being popular with your peers ☐

family happiness ☐

respect from others ☐

career progression ☐

educational qualifications ☐

money ☐

good work-life balance ☐

status in society ☐

2 Think of times when you felt demotivated. Why did you feel like this? What, if anything, made these feelings go away?

Reading strategies

A | Predicting content using the title and a diagram

1 The text you are going to read is from an academic textbook about management. Look at the title of the text and the diagram. What do you think the text is about?

2 Look at these key terms from the diagram, and the examples. Think of another example for each term.

a **Physiological** needs, e.g. *food*

_____

b **Safety** needs, e.g. *job safety*

_____

c **Belongingness** needs, e.g. *good relationship with manager*

_____

d **Esteem** needs, e.g. *status*

_____

e **Self-actualization** needs, e.g. *creativity*

_____

3 Read the text and check your ideas in 1 and 2.

4 Think back to your answers in *Study focus*. Where would you put the things that motivate you on Maslow's pyramid?

B | Reading closely for detailed information

1 Read the text again and answer the questions.

a What are the two main ideas in Maslow's theory?

b Which need is connected with creativity?

c Which need is connected with feeling you are unlikely to lose your job?

d Which need is connected with getting on well with people?

e Which need is connected with the essential things people need to stay alive?

f Which need includes being noticed by others?

g If someone has fulfilled their physiological and safety needs, can they then focus on self-actualization needs next? Why or why not?

h Why did the employees of the health-care company work there?

i Which two motivating needs were the employees currently concerned with?

2 Which need would these people want to fulfil next?

a 'I feel very secure in my role. I think there is little chance I would lose my job.'

b 'I really like all my colleagues and I have a fantastic boss.'

c 'I love the praise I get for my work and that this means I get more challenging tasks to do.'

d 'My salary is just enough for me to live on.'

C | Reacting to the text

Discuss the questions in pairs.

• Which of the needs can be met at work? Which needs are more related to private life?

• Do you agree that people should move from one need to the next? Could it be possible to leave out one of the steps? Why or why not?

• Do you think all people need to reach every stage to be satisfied?

• Many people are motivated by having more money. Where would you put this need on the pyramid?

• Think about a job you have had. Where would you put your motivation for that job on the pyramid? Why?

Maslow's Hierarchy of Needs

Probably the most famous motivation theory was developed by Abraham Maslow. Maslow's hierarchy of needs theory proposes that people are motivated by multiple needs and that these needs exist in a hierarchical order, as shown in the diagram below. Maslow named five general types of
5 motivating needs in order of importance:

1 *Physiological needs.* These most basic human physical needs include food, water, and oxygen. In the organizational setting, they are reflected in the needs for enough heat, air, and basic salary to make certain of survival.

2 *Safety needs.* These needs include a safe and secure physical and emotional
10 environment and freedom from threats – that is, for freedom from violence and for an orderly society. In an organizational workplace, safety needs reflect the needs for safe jobs, extra benefits, and job security.

3 *Belongingness needs.* These needs reflect the desire to be accepted by one's peers, have friendships, be part of a group, and be loved. In the organization,
15 these needs influence the desire for good relationships with co-workers, taking part in a work group, and a good relationship with managers.

4 *Esteem needs.* These needs relate to the desire for a good self-image and to receive attention and recognition, and be valued by others. Within organizations, esteem needs reflect a motivation for recognition, an increase
20 in responsibility, high status, and for your work to be valued.

5 *Self-actualization needs.* These include the need for self-fulfillment, which is the highest need. They concern developing one's potential, increasing one's ability, and becoming a better person. Self-actualization needs can be met in the organization by providing people with the opportunities to grow, be
25 creative, and get training for challenging tasks and advancement.

According to Maslow's theory, low-order needs take priority – they must be satisfied before high-order needs can be started.
30 The needs are satisfied in order: Physiological needs come before safety needs, safety needs before social needs, and so on. A person desiring physical safety will put
35 his or her efforts into getting a safer environment and will not be concerned with esteem needs or self-actualization needs. Once a need is satisfied, it decreases in
40 importance and the next higher need is started.

A study of employees in the manufacturing department of a big health-care company in
45 the United Kingdom provides some support for Maslow's theory. Most line workers said that they worked at the company mainly because of
50 the good pay, benefits, and job security. Thus, employees' lower-level physiological and safety needs were being met. When questioned about
55 their motivation, employees talked about the importance of positive social relationships with both peers and supervisors (belongingness needs) and a
60 desire for greater respect and recognition from management (esteem needs).

Source: R. L. Daft, *New Era of Management*, Cengage, Mason Ohio, 2009, pp507–508

Glossary

hierarchy (line 2): a system in which things are organized into levels of importance

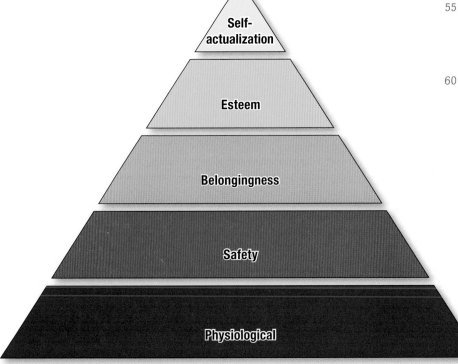

Maslow's Hierarchy of Needs

Self-actualization
Esteem
Belongingness
Safety
Physiological

Business vocabulary

A | General vocabulary

1 When reading an academic text, you need to understand three main types of vocabulary. Match the types of vocabulary a–c to definitions 1–3.

  a Academic vocabulary   ____

  b Subject-specific vocabulary   ____

  c General vocabulary   ____

  1 the vocabulary used in a particular topic or area of study

  2 the vocabulary used in any setting or situation

  3 the vocabulary used in any educational area

2 Match words and phrases a–f to definitions 1–6. Use the context of the text on page 5 to help.

  a reflect (line 12)   ____

  b desire (line 13)   ____

  c valued (line 18)   ____

  d advancement (line 25)   ____

  e according to (line 26)   ____

  f concerned with (line 37)   ____

  1 interested in

  2 a strong feeling of wanting something

  3 as stated by

  4 to show or be a sign of something

  5 progress in a job

  6 thought to be important

3 Which type of vocabulary are the words in 2?

4 Complete the summary of Maslow's theory with the words and phrases from 2. You may need to change the form of the word.

^{1}_____ Maslow's theory, there are five different levels of motivating needs. The needs at each level ^{2}_____ different ^{3}_____ , such as for good relationships with colleagues and job security. The needs are satisfied in order. Individuals are not ^{4}_____ starting a higher need until their current needs have been fully met. For example, workers need to feel that their work is ^{5}_____ by their colleagues and manager before they are interested in training for more difficult tasks and ^{6}_____ within the organization.

B | Satisfaction and development

1 Choose the correct option to complete the sentences.

  a He has a good *self-image / potential*. He is happy with his appearance and the things he has achieved in life.

  b The *ability / recognition* I get from my manager is important to me. If she praises my work, I'm motivated to work harder.

  c My car and my house are *ability / status* symbols. I want people to see that I am successful.

  d My main *potential / responsibility* is to make sure products are delivered on time.

  e He is quite a good team leader but he hasn't reached his full *potential / ability*. I think he can do better.

  f She doesn't have the *status / ability* to complete the task. I think we should give it to someone more capable.

2 Write down your answers to the questions.

  a Describe your self-image. How do you see yourself?

  _____

  _____

  b What status symbols do you own?

  _____

  _____

  c Have you reached your full potential at work or in your studies? If not, what more could you do?

  _____

  _____

  d What abilities do you need in your studies or your job?

  _____

  _____

  e In your job or a job you had in the past, what was your main responsibility?

  _____

  _____

  f Are you happy with the amount of recognition you get in your job / your studies? Why or why not?

  _____

  _____

3 In pairs, ask and answer the questions in 2.

Writing skills

A | Using relative clauses

1 Look at the example sentences. The **bold** sections are called relative clauses. Relative clauses come after the noun they refer to in a sentence and give extra information about that person or thing.

  A The teacher **who teaches Maths in our school** won an award for her teaching recently.

  B Dr Fischer, **who teaches on our physics programme**, won a Nobel Prize last year.

2 Relative clauses can be defining or non-defining. Read the definitions. Which sentence in 1 includes a defining relative clause and which includes a non-defining relative clause?

Defining clauses give extra information that is essential for identifying what the noun refers to.

Non-defining clauses give extra information that is not essential. What the noun refers to is still clear if the information is removed.

3 Which sentence, A or B, uses commas to separate the clause? Why are commas used?

4 Look at these pronouns used in relative clauses and answer questions a–c.

    that   which   who   whom   whose   where

  a Which of the pronouns are used to refer to:

    1 a person? _____

    2 a thing? _____

    3 a place? _____

    4 both a person and a thing? _____

  b Which pronoun can replace *who/which* in a defining relative clause? _____

  c Which pronoun(s) do you think are most commonly used in academic writing? Why?

5 <u>Underline</u> the relative clause in each sentence. Is it *D* (defining) or *ND* (non-defining)? Add commas to the non-defining clauses.

  a Motivation which means the need or reason for doing something is key to employee satisfaction. ____

  b Employees who worked for the central bank wanted more recognition for their work. ____

  c Employees whose safety needs are being met need to then develop good relationships at work to continue to be motivated. ____

  d Countries where unemployment is high are usually most concerned about job security. ____

B | Writing practice

1 Join the sentences together using a relative clause and the pronoun in brackets. Use commas where necessary.

  a The man introduced me to Mr Smith. He was American. (who)

    The man who introduced me to Mr Smith was American.

  b My father's company is an accountancy firm. It is in London. (which)

    _____

  c Cambridge is a fantastic city. I work there. (where)

    _____

  d I'll send you a brochure. It has all the key information. (that)

    _____

  e Our director will call you next week. I discussed the problem with her. (with whom)

    _____

2 Write sentences about terms a–c, using both defining and non-defining relative clauses. Use the text on page 5 to help.

  a motivation

    _____

    _____

  b safety needs

    _____

    _____

  c self-actualization

    _____

    _____

Research task

1 Interview one or two people you know in different companies. Find out:

  • what is important to them in their role

  • what motivates them

  • what, if anything, is missing from their role

2 Where would you put the people you interviewed on Maslow's pyramid?

3 Discuss your findings in small groups.

2 Managing conflict

Study focus

1 When did you last have a conflict with someone? What was it about? How did you resolve it?

2 Can conflict ever be positive? How?

3 How can managers at work best manage conflict between employees?

Reading strategies

A | Scanning for specific information

1 Look at the text from an academic textbook about management and answer the questions.

  a How many main sections are there?

  b What is the topic of each section?

  c How many styles are there for handling conflict?

  d Which figure shows how to balance conflict and cooperation?

2 Would you read the rest of the text to help you answer either of these essay questions?

  a Managing change is one of the main sources of conflict. Discuss.

  b Conflict, when effectively managed, is actually positive. Discuss.

B | Interpreting graphically presented data

1 Look at the two figures in the text and answer the questions.

  a Which part of the text does each figure relate to?

  b In Figure 1 what does the ball in the middle show about this team?

  c Where on Figure 1 is a team most likely to perform badly?

  d In Figure 2 which style of management is the most assertive and the least cooperative?

  e In Figure 2 which style of management is the most cooperative and least assertive?

  f The compromising style is presented in the middle of Figure 2.

    1 Using only the figure, how would you describe this style?

    2 When do you think this style might be effective?

    3 Check your answers in the text (lines 53–57).

2 Without referring to the text, write a brief summary of Figure 1. Compare your summary with the text (lines 29–40).

_____

_____

_____

_____

_____

3 It is difficult to summarize Figure 2 without looking at the text. Read lines 45–70. What extra information does the text provide?

C | Reading closely for detailed information

1 Read the text and answer the questions.

  a What are the challenges of conflict for the team leader?

  b Why does it take longer to resolve conflict in virtual teams?

  c What is groupthink?

  d Why is groupthink negative?

  e When can conflict be negative?

  f What is the effect of negative conflict?

2 Which style of handling conflict might each of these people have?

  a 'It wasn't the ideal solution, but it worked well in the short term as both sides benefited.'

  b 'The issue wasn't particularly important to me, so to avoid conflict I simply agreed with my colleague.'

  c 'I don't care about being liked. I just want to make the best decision as quickly as possible.'

  d 'The discussion took a long time, but I felt we both benefited from it.'

  e 'We needed a delay to find out more information.'

D | Reacting to the text

1 Rank the five styles for handling conflict in order from the one you would feel most comfortable doing to the one you would feel least comfortable doing.

2 Compare your rankings in pairs. Discuss your reasons.

Handling Team Conflict

Whenever people work together in teams, some conflict is inevitable. Making conflicts known and effectively resolving them is one of the team leader's most challenging, yet
5 most important jobs. For example, studies of virtual teams show that how they handle internal conflicts is critical to their success, yet conflict within virtual teams tends to happen more frequently and take longer
10 to resolve because people are separated by space, time, and cultural differences. Moreover, people in virtual teams tend to take part in more negative behaviour, such as name-calling or insults, than people who
15 work face-to-face.

Balancing conflict and cooperation

Mild conflict can actually be beneficial to teams. A healthy level of conflict helps to prevent 'groupthink', in which people are so committed to a cohesive team they are
20 unwilling to express opposite opinions. When people in work teams go along with others simply for the sake of harmony, problems usually result. Thus, a degree of conflict leads to better decision making because multiple
25 points of view are expressed. Among top management teams, for example, low levels of conflict have been found to be associated with poor decision making.

However, conflict that is too strong, that
30 is focused on personal rather than work issues, or that is not managed appropriately can be damaging to the team's morale and productivity. Too much conflict can be destructive, and interfere with the healthy
35 exchange of ideas and information. Team leaders have to find the right balance between conflict and cooperation, as shown in Figure 1 below. A moderate amount of conflict that is managed appropriately typically results in
40 the highest levels of team performance.

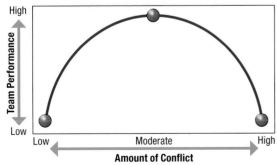

Figure 1: Balancing Conflict and Cooperation

Styles to handle conflict

Teams as well as individuals develop specific styles for dealing with conflict, based on the desire to satisfy their own concern against the other party's concern. A model that describes five styles of handling conflict can be seen in Figure 2 below.

1 The *competing style* reflects assertiveness to get one's own way. It should be used when quick, decisive action is key on important issues or unpopular actions, such as during emergencies or urgent cost cutting.

2 The *avoiding style* reflects neither assertiveness nor
50 cooperativeness. It is appropriate when an issue is not important, when there is no chance of winning, when a delay to gather information is needed, or when disruption would be costly.

3 The *compromising style* reflects a moderate amount of assertiveness and cooperativeness. It is appropriate when the goals on both sides
55 are equally important, when opponents have equal power and both sides want to compromise, or when people need to arrive at temporary solutions under time pressure.

4 The *accommodating style* reflects a high degree of cooperativeness, which works best when people realize that they
60 are wrong, when an issue is more important to others than to oneself, when building social credits for use in later discussions, and when maintaining harmony is especially important.

5 The *collaborating style* reflects both a high degree of assertiveness and cooperativeness. The collaborating style
65 enables both parties to win, although it may require substantial bargaining and negotiation. The collaborating style is important when both sets of concerns are too important to be compromised, when insights from different people need to be put together into an overall solution, and when the commitment
70 of both sides is needed for a consensus.

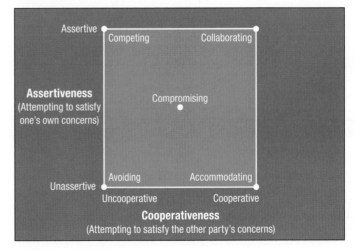

Figure 2: A Model of Styles to Handle Conflict

Source: R. L. Daft, *New Era of Management*, Cengage, Mason Ohio, 2009, pp582–584

Business vocabulary

A | Identifying parts of speech

Word endings can help to identify parts of speech. Identifying the part of speech can help to analyse a sentence and understand the meaning of the word in the text. For example:

This is a competit**ive** business to work in. Many companies do not survive.

In the example, the word ending identifies *competitive* as an adjective describing *business*. The second sentence gives an idea of the meaning.

1 Complete the table with these word endings. Some can go in more than one group.

-tion	-sion	-al	-ate	-ive	-ment	-ly	-ence
-able	-ness	-ant	-ed	-er	-age	-ship	-ism
-ity	-ous	-ful	-ize	-fy	-ing		

(*-tion* and *-ly* are crossed out; *-al* and *-ate* are crossed out)

Noun	*-tion*
Verb	*-ate*
Adjective	*-al*
Adverb	*-ly*

2 Look at these words from the text on page 9. Underline the word ending and identify the part of speech.

a inevitable (line 2) _____
b effectively (line 3) _____
c cohesive (line 19) _____
d leader (line 36) _____
e satisfy (line 42) _____

3 Match the words in 2 to definitions a–e. Use the context in the text to help work out the meaning.

a a person in charge _____
b certain to happen _____
c feeling together _____
d in a way that produces successful results _____
e to give you what you need or want _____

4 Complete the sentences with the correct form of the words in brackets.

a Conflict can be _____ (benefit) to teams as long as it is managed effectively.
b To a certain extent, conflict is a _____ (require) for a successful team.
c When people are very _____ (commit) to a cohesive team, this can have a negative effect on team performance.
d At times, _____ (cooperate) is essential. At other times, conflict is positive.
e Effective resolution of conflict is dependent on _____ (accommodate) both parties' needs.
f It is not always important or necessary to _____ (maintain) harmony.

B | Decisions and conflict

1 Match a–g to 1–7 to make collocations from the text.

a effectively ____   1 conflict
b handle ____   2 action
c cohesive ____   3 of ideas
d exchange ____   4 team
e decisive ____   5 of harmony
f overall ____   6 resolve
g degree ____   7 solution

2 Replace the phrases in *italics* with the collocations from 1.

a A *group that works together* is more effective than one that has frequent conflict.
_____

b They managed to *find a satisfactory solution to* the problem. _____

c Although conflict is positive, the team needs a *certain amount of peace* to be effective.
_____

d He needs to focus on the *best way to solve the whole problem* not on minor details.
_____

e She is able to *deal with disagreement* in an effective way. _____

f The *sharing of thoughts* can result in new ways of dealing with problems. _____

g We don't need ongoing discussion; we need a *quick decision*. _____

Writing skills

A | Using present and past simple tenses

Present and past simple tenses are commonly used in academic texts to discuss facts, general truths or states.

1 Look back at the text on page 9 and <u>underline</u> all the different verb forms. Which tense is used most often?

2 There are three main uses of the present simple. Match sentences 1–3 to uses a–c.

a present state ____
b repeated action/habit ____
c general truth ____

1 Whenever people work together in teams, some conflict is inevitable.
2 … people in virtual teams tend to take part in more negative behaviour, such as name-calling …
3 The team is in danger of breaking down.

3 Which use of the present simple is the most common in the text on page 9?

4 <u>Underline</u> the verb forms in this text. Which tense is used?

The company dealt with many challenges when it merged last year. Two very different cultures existed in the two companies. The company culture in one organization was very hierarchical, which had an impact on how they ran and chaired meetings. The managers from this company didn't expect much contribution from subordinates at meetings.

5 Past tenses are used less frequently than present simple tenses, partly because they have fewer uses. Look at the verbs you underlined in 4 and match them to these uses.

a past action

_____
_____
_____

b past habit/state

_____
_____
_____

6 Complete the sentences with the correct form of the verbs in brackets.

a Throughout the merger, the team _____ (suffer) due to a lack of commitment from their leader.
b Teams as well as individuals usually _____ (develop) specific styles for dealing with conflict.
c The competing style of management _____ (reflect) the desire to get one's own way.
d Everyone _____ (cooperate) to such an extent that 'groupthink' became an issue.
e This theory is unlikely to be true in all cultures, especially cultures that _____ (value) collective harmony above individual goals.
f The management style _____ (fail) during the recent cost cutting because an avoiding style _____ (be) used in a situation that _____ (require) a competing style.

B | Writing practice

1 Write three sentences about your views on appropriate behaviour when people work together in teams.

_____
_____
_____
_____

2 Write three sentences about a team or group conflict that happened at work or your place of study.

_____
_____
_____
_____

Research task

Think of different situations when you have used styles similar to those described in the text.

Was this the most effective style for the situation? Why or why not?

Would you feel comfortable using all the different styles? Or would one be more natural for you?

Discuss your ideas in small groups.

3 Work-life balance

Study focus

1 What is the one main change that has affected work-life balance in the last 40 years?

2 Whose responsibility is it to maintain a good work-life balance?

families   individuals   companies   managers

3 What are the positive and negative effects for companies when they increase employee workloads?

Reading strategies

A | Reading quickly for general understanding

1 Read the text from an academic textbook about working life. Which statement a–c completes this summary best?

The text describes the fact that the …
a average American working week has got longer since the 1960s.
b average American company expects more work from each individual.
c average American family roles have changed and placed more pressure on each family.

2 Match topics a–d to paragraphs A–D in the text.

a Time pressure: past and present ____
b Americans are not working longer ____
c The change in men's and women's roles ____
d Household working hours ____

B | Identifying the writer's point of view

1 Read the text again. Circle *T* (true) or *F* (false).

According to the point of view of the writer …
a time pressure is an issue in America.   T / F
b changes in work-life balance have affected men the most.   T / F
c Schor's claim about the average length of the working week is true.   T / F
d working hours of individuals have changed.   T / F

2 Which statement is the best summary of the writer's opinion on work-life balance?

a Individuals are working longer hours and this is putting more pressure on them.
b Families now work more combined paid hours and this is the main cause of poor work-life balance.
c Women now work more hours and men work fewer hours. This change is causing pressure on relationships.
d Increased wealth will allow families to have a better work-life balance.

C | Summarizing a text to focus on main ideas

1 Discuss the questions in pairs.

a What does a good summary of a text contain?
b Why is it a good idea to write a summary from notes and not directly from the text?

2 Look at the notes on paragraph A of the text. Then read the example summary based on the notes.

Balance – family, work + free time
Schor's 'Overworked American' = much public discussion of topic
More people feel rushed today
1965 = 24% feel rushed
1992 = 38% //   //

Schor's *Overworked American* created much discussion on the balance of work, family life and free time. Today, more people feel rushed with an increase from 24% to 38% between 1965 and 1992.

3 Identify the main ideas to summarize in paragraphs B–D.

D | Reacting to the text

Discuss the questions in pairs.

• Has work-life balance become more of an issue in your country? What effect is it having on family life?
• Who is responsible for making sure people have a good work-life balance? Individuals, companies or governments?

Has it become harder to balance work and family life?

A Today's debates about work-life balance are mainly about how to manage time – time for work, time for caring for family members, and enough free time. Since the publication of Schor's *The Overworked American*
5 (1991), the politics of working time has become a central issue in economics, industrial relations, and the sociology of work and gender relations. Schor's argument, also made by many others (Hochschild 1997; Galinksy 1999), that US workers are spending more
10 time at work than their parents and grandparents, was recognized as true by many people. Whereas economic progress and increased wealth were supposed to deliver more free time, the lack of free time is a growing concern related to the quality of modern
15 family life. Time pressure is now a common experience. This is shown by the fact that an increasing per cent of the population feel short of time. Starting in 1965, the US time-use researcher John Robinson and his team have been asking people: 'Would you say you always
20 feel rushed, even to do things you have to do, only sometimes feel rushed, or almost never feel rushed?' The proportion of 18–64-year-olds who reported 'always' feeling rushed rose from 24 per cent in 1965 to 38 per cent in 1992; it then declined slightly in 1995
25 (Robinson and Godbey 1997:231). Time poverty is particularly experienced by women who balance work, family, and free time.

B In the past, the traditional division of labour between men and women was influenced by the role of men and
30 women. Marriage and work organization was based around the separation of public life from home life. Women's main responsibility was for domestic duties, while men specialized in paid work. Men were seen as the breadwinners, working full-time outside the home,
35 and therefore doing little domestic work. Whereas men's identity primarily came through their job, women's was said to be based on their roles as wives and mothers. There was a relationship between these work patterns and the patriarchal family form.

C Surprisingly, there is little empirical evidence supporting Schor's claim that the average length of the work week has changed appreciably in recent decades. Indeed, Robinson and Godbey (1997) argue that between 1965 and 1995, free time actually increased
45 (also see Gershuny 2000). So how do we account for this mismatch with people's experience of a fall in family time?

D What happens to individuals' average hours of work is not the same as what happens to households.
50 As Jacobs and Gerson (2004) have pointed out, discussions about average working hours hides a large redistribution of paid work between the sexes (see also Epstein and Kalleberg 2004). While the contribution of prime-age men has significantly
55 declined, the hours that prime-age women contribute to the labour market have significantly increased. It is as if much of the paid work has been transferred from men to women. The resulting two-income households are supplying more working hours to the
60 labour market than ever before. Time pressure is especially strong in families with children, where both husband and wife are in full-time employment. The perception that life has become more rushed is due to the increases in the combined work commitments.
65 It is not due to the changes in the working time of individual workers. This change in family roles and gender relations over the last few decades is the key to explaining the shortage of family time.

Source: P. Edwards & J. Wajcman, *The Politics of Working Life*, 2005, Oxford University Press, Oxford, pp44–47

Glossary

breadwinner (line 34): main income earner in a household
patriarchal (line 39): ruled or controlled by men

Business vocabulary

A | The working environment

1 Match collocations a–h from the text on page 13 to meanings 1–8.

   a industrial relations (line 6) ____
   b economic progress (line 11/12) ____
   c increased wealth (line 12) ____
   d main responsibility (line 32) ____
   e paid work (line 33) ____
   f average hours (line 48) ____
   g working hours (line 51) ____
   h full-time employment (line 62) ____

   1 a job for which money is earned
   2 the time which you spend doing your job
   3 advances made in areas such as finance and business
   4 to have one main job that takes a complete working week
   5 a greater amount of money
   6 the most important role, function or task
   7 the typical length of a working week in a country or sector
   8 the dealings of a company with its employees and the public

2 Complete the text with collocations from 1.

The ¹_____ in a typical working week in the UK are approximately 40 hours for ²_____ . Both adults in many families contribute to the labour market and are in ³_____ outside the home. This has resulted in ⁴_____ and a higher standard of living. However, many families are time poor as they try to balance more ⁵_____ in employment and the domestic duties which were traditionally the ⁶_____ of the woman. It was believed that ⁷_____ would give people more free time, but this has not been the case for many people.

B | Time

1 Many words collocate with *time*. Find phrases in the text on page 13 to match definitions a–d.

   a to organize your time in order to complete a variety of tasks or roles (para. A)

   _____

   b to feel that you do not have enough time (para. A)

   _____

   c time spent at work (para. D)

   _____

   d to feel stress on your family time, typically because work takes too much of your time (para. D)

   _____

2 Rewrite the sentences so that the meaning is the same, using collocations from sections A1 and B1.

   a Many people feel that they do not have enough time with their family.

   Many people have a shortage of family time.

   b The most important part of my role is managing key accounts.

   My _____

   _____ .

   c Academic study involves organizing a schedule to meet a variety of deadlines.

   Academic _____

   _____ .

   d How the company acts with its employees is an important part of its philosophy.

   The _____

   _____ .

   e Many charities cannot afford to provide a salary for their employees and rely on voluntary workers.

   Charities _____

   _____ .

Writing skills

A | Connecting ideas

1 Words that connect ideas within a text typically have four functions. Complete the table with these words and phrases.

previously   in addition   results in   both   due to
for instance   whereas   first

Related ideas and examples	*furthermore*
Sequence	*secondly*
Contrast/Comparison	*however*
Cause/Effect	*therefore*

2 Look at these sentences from the text on page 13. What is the function of each word in **bold**?

a **Whereas** men's identity primarily came through their job, women's was said to be based on their roles as wives and mothers.

b The perception that life has become more rushed is **due to** the increases in the combined work commitments.

c Men were seen as the breadwinners, working full-time outside the home, and **therefore** doing little domestic work.

B | Writing practice

1 Complete the sentences with a suitable connecting word from section A1.

a According to Robinson and Godby (1997), in 1965 24% of people felt rushed, _____ in 1992 38% felt rushed.

b More women work today and _____ families as a whole are under more pressure in terms of time.

c A key issue for two-income families is how to manage time, _____ time for work, time for caring for children and free time for themselves.

d In the past, men were seen as the main income earner. Today, _____ , both husband and wife are often in full-time employment.

2 Look at the information below. Link the ideas together in a short text using connecting words from section A1. Start with:

The average working week has changed considerably in recent years.

- In 1962 men worked an average of 52 hours per week.
- In 1999 men worked an average of 40 hours per week.
- In 1950 10% of women had paid work.
- In 2000 75% of women had paid work.
- In 1955 2% of men were mainly responsible for the domestic household.
- In 2005 20% of men were mainly responsible for the domestic household.
- The average household in 1950 worked 52 hours per week.
- The average household in 2005 worked 70 hours per week.
- Households today are under more time pressure.

C | Spelling and punctuation

1 Which word in each group is spelt correctly?

a benifit definitely breif beleive originaly

b alowed arival disapprove polution arange

c intresting listning yesteday diffrent wonderful

d desparate appearence simlar gaurantee prefer

e their beleif releif peir greif

2 Identify the punctuation mistake in each sentence and correct it.

a The english language is the most spoken language in the world.

b The current recession has it's roots in the credit crunch of 2007/08.

c After selling the business he managed to avoid bankruptcy.

d Jonathan Sayer, the director, of the company, resigned, from his position.

e Maria Stuart dressed in the grey suit is the director of the company.

Research task

Choose two companies you know about and investigate their policies on work-life balance. Compare and contrast the differences in their policies. Which company's policies match your own views on work-life balance?

4 Financial crisis

Study focus

1 Make a list of different types of crisis, e.g. *an earthquake*.

2 Compare your list with a partner. Are any of your ideas related to the world of business?

3 What is a *financial crisis*?

Reading strategies

A | Understanding a text using background knowledge

Topics that are familiar are usually easier to understand. Thinking about your general knowledge on a topic first can help you understand a text.

1 In pairs, discuss what you know about topics a–f. Include any personal experience you have of them.

  a stock markets
  b recession
  c speculation
  d types of financial asset
  e the 'credit crunch' of 2007/08
  f the US sub-prime lending market

2 Read the text from an academic textbook about international business. Which paragraphs contain the topics in 1?

3 How similar is your knowledge to the information in the text? Rate each topic in 1 out of 5.

very different 1 2 3 4 5 very similar

4 How much did your knowledge help you understand the text? Rate yourself out of 5.

Not at all 1 2 3 4 5 A lot

B | Identifying points to support an argument

Read the text again. Tick (✓) the argument which is true for each paragraph.

  A 1 Financial crisis cannot be explained by a theory.
     2 Financial crisis happens because of speculation.
  B 1 Markets are predictable.
     2 Markets are unpredictable.

  C 1 Lending to people with poor credit histories was the cause of the 2007 crisis.
     2 Banks borrowing more money against mortgage loans was the cause of the 2007 crisis.
  D 1 Everyone knew where the greatest risk was.
     2 No one knew where the greatest risk was.

C | Finding support for an opinion

An academic text can be used to inform your opinion and to strengthen arguments in your own writing.

1 Read the two opinions. Which is stronger and why?

  a It is inevitable that price increases will eventually lead to a fall in prices.
  b A rise in prices is often followed by a fall in prices. According to Stiglitz (2002), this is because the optimism of a boom is often followed by extreme negative feelings in a recession.

2 <u>Underline</u> the part of the text that supports opinions a–e.

  a People speculate on a wide variety of assets. (para. A)
  b People begin to feel certain that prices will keep rising. (para. B)
  c Once prices start to fall, people's behaviour and the consequences change quickly. (para. B)
  d Banks will often lend more money in a rising market. (para. C)
  e Government needed to support the market. (para. D)

D | Reacting to the text

Discuss the questions in pairs.

- Do you think anyone in particular was to blame for the 2007 credit crunch, e.g. banks, governments, individuals?
- Do you think financial crises will always happen or can they be prevented?

Financial crises

A There is no generally accepted theory to explain the causes of financial crises but one thing is sure, they happen again and again. They involve speculation when assets are bought, in the hope that the price will
5 rise, or sold, in the expectation of a fall in the price. If the price rises, those who bought the asset can sell and make a profit. If the price falls, sellers can profit by buying the asset back at a lower price. The objects of speculation can be financial assets such as shares,
10 bonds, or currencies, or physical assets such as land, property, or works of art. Crises happen when the speculation destabilizes the market causing prices to rise or fall dramatically.

B Galbraith (1990) and Stiglitz (2002) examine how during
15 times of speculation, 'bubbles' develop. When an asset is increasing in price it attracts new buyers who think that prices will continue to rise. This increases demand for the asset and its price goes up. With prices increasing fast, investors come in to take advantage
20 of the easy profits to be made. Euphoria develops as people start to believe that the upward movement in prices will always continue. As the value of the asset rises, investors are able to use it as security to borrow money from the banks to buy more of the
25 asset. However, inevitably, there comes a turning point where some people decide to leave the market. The resulting fall in prices causes panic in the market with investors rushing to off-load their assets leading to a market collapse. Stiglitz (2002) makes the point
30 that the high levels of optimism or euphoria caused by bubbles is often followed by times of extreme pessimism and recession. Financial crises spread easily both domestically and internationally. For example, a banking crisis can make borrowing more difficult
35 and costly for firms and consumers. This could cause them to reduce their demand for products and services leading to bankruptcies and increasing unemployment. In an increasingly connected world, a financial crisis in one country can very quickly spread to others as
40 happened during the South East Asian crisis of the late 1990s and the credit crunch of 2007.

In summary, financial crises are characterized by:
- an increase in speculative activity, market euphoria, and rapidly rising prices;
45 - a turning point which leads to panic selling, extreme pessimism, and rapidly decreasing prices;
- spreading to domestic and foreign economies.

C The credit crunch of 2007/08 has the same characteristics as a lot of other financial crises. There
50 was much speculative activity in the US property market. House prices were rising and financial institutions were happy to lend to borrowers with poor credit histories. But lenders did not keep these sub-prime mortgages on their books. On the strength
55 of the future income from loans, they borrowed more money by issuing bonds which they sold to other financial institutions in the USA and abroad. This is called securitization. However, the bonds were based not simply on the high-risk mortgages but were put
60 together with other financial products of varying risk.

D Like any other security, the bonds were used by their buyers to raise loans. However, when US interest rates rose and house prices fell, many borrowers couldn't pay the money back. The value of the securities dropped
65 rapidly and the market euphoria disappeared as banks faced up to big losses. Because mortgages had been sold in combination with other products, no one could be quite sure about the distribution of risk. As a result, there was a crisis of liquidity. Banks were unwilling to
70 lend to each other because they couldn't find out which banks were carrying most risk. The crisis spread very rapidly across markets and continents. Banks wrote off large amounts of assets and central banks had to put in billions of dollars to prevent the credit system
75 from failing completely. Banks were taken into public ownership in the USA, UK, the Netherlands, France, Iceland and Portugal. Indeed the Icelandic government was forced to go to the IMF for a loan.

Source: L. Hamilton & P. Webster, *The International Business Environment*, Oxford University Press, Oxford, 2009, pp294–296

Glossary

euphoria (line 20): extreme happiness with a situation
mortgage (line 54): a loan made to someone for the purpose of buying a house

Business vocabulary

A | Verb + preposition collocation

In English there are a lot of **verb + preposition** collocations. You can understand the meaning if you know the meaning of both the verb and preposition.

1 Match sentence beginnings a–e to endings 1–5.

   a Financial crises are *characterized*   ____

   b Many governments had to *put*   ____

   c A banking crisis in one country can quickly *spread*   ____

   d The recent recession was *caused*   ____

   e This crisis was caused partly by high-risk mortgages being *put*   ____

   1 *in* funds to prevent the banks from collapsing.

   2 *by* speculation, rapidly rising prices and then sudden panic.

   3 *together* with other products, so no one knew where the main risk was.

   4 *across* markets and continents.

   5 *by* the sudden fall in house prices.

2 Match the collocations in *italics* in 1 to meanings a–e.

   a move something into a place

   b made to happen

   c combine two or more things into one single thing

   d cover a larger and larger area

   e showing the typical features of something

B | Phrasal verbs

Sometimes when a preposition is added to a verb, the meaning of the verb is changed. This is called a **phrasal verb**.

1 Match phrasal verbs a–e to meanings 1–5. Use the context in the text on page 17 to help.

   a base on (line 58/59)   ____

   b pay back (line 63/64)   ____

   c face up to (line 66)   ____

   d find out (line 70)   ____

   e write off (line 72/73)   ____

   1 say that money owed no longer has to be paid

   2 use a fact or situation to develop something else

   3 return money to the person who lent or gave it to you

   4 accept or handle a difficult situation or problem

   5 discover

2 Complete the sentences with a verb + preposition or a phrasal verb from sections A and B.

   a The financial crisis in Thailand was _____ speculation in the property market.

   b The bank had to _____ the debt because borrowers with poor credit histories could no longer pay their mortgages.

   c The government had to _____ the difficult economic situation and try to deal with it.

   d The rise in IT related shares was _____ many of the features of other stock booms.

   e Various financial products were _____ _____ to form an attractive deal.

   f Many rises in share prices are _____ the belief that the price will continue to rise.

   g The banking crisis quickly _____ the USA and most of Europe.

   h The lender will check that the borrower has the ability to _____ the loan.

C | Finance

1 Complete the sentences by choosing the correct word in brackets for each gap.

   a A [1]_____ is one of the equal parts of a company that you can buy. A [2]_____ is a document from a government or company promising to pay a fixed rate of interest on money invested. (bond, share)

   b A person who takes an amount of money as a [1]_____ from a bank is a [2]_____ . (borrower, loan)

   c Bonds that have a higher interest rate usually have a greater [1]_____ because there is more chance of suffering [2]_____ if interest rates rise and the value of the bond decreases. (losses, risk)

   d Having enough money can be a problem for small businesses. These possible [1]_____ problems can lead to many [2]_____ where businesses are unable to pay what they owe. (bankruptcies, liquidity)

2 A well-known financial expression in English is:

Neither a borrower nor a lender be.

In pairs, discuss what you think this expression means and whether you agree with it or not.

Writing skills

A | Writing a descriptive text

Descriptive writing does not include an opinion. It is used for describing processes, describing objects and defining topics. Descriptive language often includes adjectives, present simple verbs and passive forms.

1 Match the types of descriptive writing a–c to examples 1–3.

   a Describing a process ____
   b Describing an object ____
   c Defining a topic ____

   1 Physical assets can include items such as a house, a car, buildings or land.
   2 Lenders provided people with a poor credit history with loans. They subsequently put these together with loans that were considered to be less of a risk. This package was then sold to another institution.
   3 Economics is the way in which money, trade and industry are organized.

2 The text on page 17 is mostly descriptive. It describes a process and defines topics. Look at this extract from the text.

   The credit crunch … has the same characteristics as a lot of other financial crises. There was much speculative activity in the US property market. House prices were rising and financial institutions were happy to lend to borrowers with poor credit histories.

   Choose the correct option.

   a The *highlighted / underlined* words describe a process.
   b The *highlighted / underlined* words define topics.

3 Adjectives are used to help define topics in descriptive writing. Use the context of the text on page 17 to match adjectives a–f to definitions 1–6.

   a extreme (line 31) ____
   b speculative (line 43) ____
   c domestic (line 47) ____
   d sub-prime (line 54) ____
   e high-risk (line 59) ____
   f public (line 75) ____

   1 owned by the government
   2 very large in amount
   3 relating to a person's own country
   4 buying in the hope of making a profit in the future
   5 below the average level
   6 not very secure

4 Look at this sentence from the text and answer the questions below.

   Financial crises spread easily both domestically and internationally.

   a Underline the verb. What tense is it?
   b What is the function of the verb in the sentence? Does the writer believe he is writing about *facts / something that is generally true*?

5 Look at these two sentences from the text.

   A Banks were taken into public ownership in the USA, UK, the Netherlands, France, Iceland and Portugal.
   B But lenders did not keep these sub-prime mortgages on their books.

   a Underline the verb in each sentence. How does the verb form differ between the two sentences?
   b Sentence A uses the passive form. Use this sentence to explain how the passive is structured.
   c Do we know who took the banks into public ownership in sentence A? Do we know who did not keep the sub-prime mortgages on their books in B?

   Passive structures are used when the focus of the sentence is on what is being done or happening rather than who is completing the action.

6 Complete the sentences with the present simple active or passive form of the verbs in brackets.

   a Market euphoria _____ (cause) by a belief that prices will continue to rise.
   b Many individuals do not have the ability to pay back money they have borrowed so the debt _____ (write) off.
   c The rise in prices _____ (base) on speculation not real value.
   d Lenders _____ (issue) bonds so they can borrow more money.

B | Writing practice

Using present simple active or passive and appropriate adjectives do the following.

1 Define *speculation*.
2 Describe the causes of a financial crisis.
3 Describe the New York Stock Exchange.

Research task

Research another financial crisis from the past. Write a brief description of what happened during the crisis. Share your information in small groups.

5 Marketing

Study focus

1 What influences you when you buy something? Rate each of the following out of 5 (1 = a lot, 5 = not at all).

price   brand   quality   convenience   familiarity

2 How does a company target its products at a particular group of people?

3 What do you think would be the typical car and holiday for the following age groups?

18+   30+   50+

Reading strategies

A | Identifying topic sentences

A topic sentence contains the main idea of a paragraph. Everything else in the paragraph is related to this sentence.

1 Read the text from an academic textbook about marketing. Underline the topic sentence in each paragraph.

2 Referring to the topic sentence, tick (✓) the best summary for the main idea in each paragraph.

   A 1 Consumers are all individuals and therefore cannot be grouped.
     2 Consumers have different characteristics and these are targeted by companies.
   B 1 Age has an effect on consumers.
     2 Gender has an effect on consumers.
   C 1 Matching multiple brands to different age groups is an effective strategy.
     2 One brand can effectively fit all age groups.
   D 1 Age has an effect on consumer behaviour, but it's quite minor.
     2 Age has the biggest effect on consumer behaviour.

3 Suggest a rule for the position of the topic sentence in a paragraph.

_____

_____

_____

B | Identifying main and supporting ideas

Each topic sentence or main idea is generally supported by one or more of the following.

Details: *Above all, it has the advantage of being simple, real and easy to use in terms of media planning.*

Examples: *For example, it is quite clear the consumption of health products or services are connected very strongly with biological age.*

Explanation: *When age is used as the central criterion for segmentation, one realises that it is in fact statistically the best way to design a reasonably accurate model of the targeted consumer.*

Supporting sentences often make the main idea clearer.

Read each paragraph in the text again. Underline the supporting sentences. Which type of support – details, examples or explanation – is used in each paragraph?

C | Drawing conclusions from a text

1 Read the conclusions a–d that can be drawn from the paragraphs in the text. Match each conclusion to the correct paragraph.

   a Age is the most effective criterion for a company to plan its marketing strategy. ___
   b Everybody is influenced in their purchasing by who they are and marketers target this. ___
   c If a company chooses an effective strategy to target their consumers, sales can grow and even lead to the company becoming a market leader. ___
   d Companies with a wide product range can be successful by targeting each product at one consumer group. ___

2 Tick (✓) the main conclusion that can be drawn from the text.

   a Consumers are targeted in many ways by different companies.
   b Age is the most effective way to target consumers.
   c Companies that differentiate their marketing are the most successful.

D | Reacting to the text

Do you think your age affects your purchases? Give some examples.

The importance of age over all other segmentation criteria

A Every product or service is aimed at a group of target consumers with particular characteristics. This is because products assume some moment in the consumer's routine, culture or knowledge, or even
5 the approval of society. One method of targeting is via age, which can be divided into two main areas: biological (actual) age and psychological (mental) age. For example, it is quite clear the consumption of health products or services are connected very strongly with
10 biological age. On the other hand, the consumption of cultural services, such as the theatre or literature, will be much more influenced by the psychological age.

B Age has a noticeable effect on the needs of consumers in many areas. On the other hand, other markets stay
15 fairly similar throughout life, such as food products, for example, since we all need to eat. But even for a market that involves everyone, segmentation by age is often important because it allows for more precise, and therefore more effective, marketing and advertising.
20 An example is the lower-fat cheese range from the Bongrain Group in France called 'Fine Bouche', which is supposed to be aimed at everyone. Some years after it first entered the French market, the brand discovered it was selling more among the over 50s, who
25 found in this product the right balance between taste and lightness (health concerns are always stronger among the over 50s than in any other age group). The company decided to take advantage of this by making a TV 'infomercial' designed to interest directly the
30 over 50s and broadcast only during the day over two TV channels with many 50+ viewers. With a very modest budget (about 300,000 euros per year), sales volumes increased by 40% in the months following the campaign. Thanks to this strategic choice, the brand
35 became leader of its market sector in two years.

C In the USA, from the 1920s while the Model T Ford had 55% of the car market, General Motors chose a very different strategy to divide its brands according to the age of its customers. The idea was that for each
40 stage of a person's life there was a price range, together with a certain standard of comfort and equipment. This strategy was presented as 'A car for every purse and every purpose'. Each brand had its target age of consumer, from the cheapest Chevrolet (for the young
45 and less well off), through the Pontiac, Oldsmobile, Buick, up to the top of the range, with the Cadillac (for the old and rich). When a person is young, a car must present a certain image and at the same time have room to take friends. Later, it must accommodate
50 child seats and frequent trips to the supermarket. Afterwards, it must show that one has reached a certain social status while still allowing for issues such as safety, comfort and size. All of this matches the majority of car buyers' behaviour in 2002, including
55 more unusual behaviour that is beginning to appear, for example, those over 50s who go for the smart 'young' small cars, such as the Twingo from Renault, the Yaris from Toyota, or even the Smart.

D Every marketing manager is always looking for the
60 most relevant and operational criteria for building a target market. It is quite clear that age is one, if not the key, criterion that drives consumer behaviour. Above all, it has the advantage of being simple, real and easy to use in terms of media planning. Simplicity is a basic
65 virtue in marketing! When age is used as the central criterion for segmentation one realises that it is in fact statistically the best way to design a reasonably accurate model of the targeted consumer. It will therefore be relatively easy for the marketing manager
70 to think about the economic situation, financial resources, main needs as to equipment and services, preferred shops, the best time to advertise, and so on.

Source: J.P. Treguer, *50+ Marketing*, Palgrave, Basingstoke, 2002, pp12–14

Glossary

allow for (line 18): make possible

infomercial (line 29): an advertisement that also aims to inform or educate the consumer

Business vocabulary

A | Marketing and segmentation

1 Replace the words and phrases in *italics* with these words.

characteristic   segmentation   enter   trend
campaign   strategy   image   target
consumer

a The *division* of markets into different groups enables companies to create advertising that appeals to a particular group. _____

b It can be difficult for a company to *go into* a market in a country or culture that it hasn't worked in before. _____

c It is vital for a company to have a *detailed plan* for achieving growth and financial success. _____

d Companies try to *aim* their marketing at particular groups of people. _____

e The *general development* in retail has been for more shopping to be done online. _____

f One *feature* of the fifty plus market is that it has more disposable income. _____

g It is important to organize a *planned group of activities* to help sell a product. _____

h The *thoughts people have* of a product will influence who is likely to buy it. _____

i The *customer* is key to any company but especially in the service industry. _____

2 Use the words from 1 and your own ideas to write sentences about a–i.

a the characteristics of drivers of a type of car

Drivers of four-by-four cars either usually have large families or work in the farming industry.

b the segmentation of a particular industry

c a company that has entered a market recently

d a recent consumer trend

e an advertising campaign you thought was good

f the strategy of a company to position itself within a market

g the image of a well-known company

h who the target market is for a well-known product

i who the main consumers are of a particular product

B | Noun + *of* + noun

One of the most common vocabulary patterns in academic writing is **noun +** *of* **+ noun**, e.g. *group of consumers*. Each phrase has its own meaning, so you need to recognize it as a group of words rather than individual words with separate meanings.

1 Match phrases a–g from the text on page 21 to definitions 1–7.

a approval of society (line 5) ___

b consumption of products and services (line 8/9) ___

c needs of consumers (line 13) ___

d leader of its market sector (line 35) ___

e stage of a person's life (line 40) ___

f standard of comfort (line 41) ___

g target age of consumer (line 43/44) ___

1 the purchase and use of different things

2 a point or period of time for an individual

3 the desires or wants of customers

4 a certain level that is required to make a person feel at ease or relaxed

5 the positive opinion of a group of people

6 the particular generation of customers that a product is aimed at

7 the top or main company in a particular field or industry

2 Complete the text with the phrases from 1.

The ¹_____ – what consumers actually buy and why – is influenced by a number of factors. Some purchases are affected by the ²_____ , such as how much space is required in a family car or a particular ³_____ with a sofa. For some people, the ⁴_____ is important and they buy things because they want to be accepted or recognized as having a particular status. One of the biggest influences on purchases is the age of the consumer. The kinds of products that are desired and purchased often reflect a ⁵_____ , such as the teenage years or parenthood. Companies are well aware of all these factors and will base their marketing strategy on a number of criteria, with ⁶_____ being one of the most important. A company that successfully understands its target group and implements a strategy well has the potential to become a ⁷_____ .

Writing skills

A | Writing comparisons

1 Look at lines 8–12 in the text on page 21. What two things are compared? Underline the comparative language.

2 Use the comparative language you underlined in the text to complete this sentence.

Social class is considered an important criterion for targeting a consumer. _____ , it can be argued that gender is a _____ important criteria.

3 What is compared in lines 13–19 in the text on page 21? Underline the comparative language.

4 Use comparative language you underlined in the text to complete this sentence.

People from the same social class will purchase _____ products. However, a _____ effective criterion to determine behaviour is age.

5 Complete the table with these words and phrases for describing similarities and differences.

in contrast to   neither … nor   as … as   whereas
compared with   in comparison with   instead
similarly   on the other hand   also   rather   both

Similarities	likewise
Differences	however

6 Complete the sentences with words and phrases from 5.

a This year, the company's profits were _____ good _____ its rival's.

b _____ the British economy, the Chinese economy continues to grow.

c 400 million people speak English as a first language _____ 1.4 billion speak it as a second language.

d China is a growing economy. _____ so is India.

e _____ than go to university for education, many people go simply to get a better job.

7 Choose two products you know well that are similar and two that are different. Write a short comparison of the products, explaining their similarities and differences.

B | Writing topic sentences

As discussed on page 20, a topic sentence gives the main idea of a paragraph.

1 Match these topic sentences to paragraphs 1 and 2.

a Understanding the market has additional complications in today's global world. ___

b Every company targets its consumers by using segmentation criteria. ___

1 For example, age, gender, social class and profession. These criteria are then used to choose the method of advertising to shape the marketing campaign. The successful development of both is key to a company's success in its market.

2 Cultural values and attitudes will impact on buying behaviour and therefore segmentation of consumers. Misunderstanding these differences can be detrimental to a company's success.

2 In pairs, discuss the main idea of each of these paragraphs. Then use your ideas to write a topic sentence.

a _____

So to be able to operate in an international context, a basic knowledge of English is essential. However, 90% of trade conducted in English does not involve native speakers. Therefore, arguably, native-like fluency is not necessary.

b _____

It is the most consumed soft drink and one of the most recognizable brands in the world. Some even argue that the company owns the colour red, ever since it changed the traditional green costume of Father Christmas from green to red. Part of the company's success comes from its ability to adapt to local markets, without which it may still just be an American soft drink.

Research task

Choose two similar markets that are aimed at different consumers. Write a short comparison discussing the similarities and giving details of the products and their consumers.

Study focus

1 What are the stereotypes of people from your country?

2 Are the people of any other countries thought to be quite similar to your country?

3 Which countries are very different from your country? What makes these countries different? Think about things such as food, religion, politics, business, language.

Reading strategies

A | Predicting content using titles and topic sentences

1 The text you are going to read is from an academic textbook about international business. Look at the title of the text. What do you think the text is about?

   a Societies of the world

   b How society and culture are organized

   c Intercultural education

2 Read the topic sentence below for each paragraph in the text. What do you think the paragraph is about? After each prediction, read the paragraph to check your ideas.

   A Culture can be seen as a system of shared beliefs, values, customs, and behaviours common in society and that are passed from generation to generation (Bates and Plog, 1990).

   B Cultural attitudes can have important implications for business.

   C Research has shown major cultural differences between East and West that are important for Western business people trying to do business in the East.

   D Researchers think this is caused by different social environments.

   E Cultural differences influence the way firms in the East and West do business.

   F The result is that business has to take cultural differences into account when considering entry to foreign markets through exports, joint ventures, or through takeovers.

B | Reading closely for detailed information

Read the text again and answer the questions.

1 What different things are part of culture?

2 Who did Hofstede study and what did he find out?

3 What is the main difference between Eastern and Western people in how they see the world around them?

4 What is the reason for this difference?

5 How do cultural differences affect the way business is done in different countries?

6 What should a company pay attention to when entering different international markets?

C | Using the text in writing

1 Which of these essay questions would the text be most useful for?

   a Globalization is having a negative impact on the diversity of cultures in the world. Discuss.

   b Without local knowledge a company will not be able to enter new international markets successfully. To what extent do you agree with this statement?

2 Underline the parts of the text you could use to support these opinions.

   a Culture forms part of any society around the world and is continually changing even more so today than in the past.

   b Culture not only influences people in social situations, it also plays a large role in influencing behaviour in the working world.

   c Culture does not have to be associated with one particular country, especially in countries that cover a large geographical area.

   d There are particularly strong differences in how people from the East and West of the planet view the world.

   e Countries that have a culture that is similar will be easier to operate in.

D | Reacting to the text

Discuss the questions in pairs.

- What differences do you know of between your culture and other cultures in the world?

- Are there any cultures that might be difficult for companies from your culture to operate in?

The socio-cultural framework

A Culture can be seen as a system of shared beliefs, values, customs, and behaviours common in society and that are passed from generation to generation (Bates and Plog, 1990). Hofstede (1994),
5 the management scientist, described these parts of culture as the software of the mind, 'the collective programming of the mind which distinguishes the members of one category of people from another'. The values in the culture are enforced by a set of rules of
10 behaviour. A set of controls is usually added to these rules to make sure they are respected. Culture is made up of many different features, including religion, language, non-verbal communication, food, dress, and institutions to make sure that the values and beliefs
15 are passed from one generation to another. Culture is dynamic, in other words it changes over time especially due to the process of globalization with the increasing movement of products, services, and capital between countries, and the migration of people (Dahl).

B Cultural attitudes can have important implications for business. Some of the most influential research on culture and work was carried out by Hofstede (1991; 2001). His study, the largest that had then been done, surveyed over 100,000 workers in IBM companies
25 in 40 countries looking for cultural explanations of differences in employee attitude and behaviour. He concluded that the rules and values set in national culture were a very powerful influence on the workplace, and that different approaches would be
30 necessary when managing people from different cultural backgrounds. Hofstede (1994) concludes that the workplace can only change people's values in a limited way. The message for multinational companies was not to assume that an organizational culture that
35 was successful in the cultural context, for example of the USA, would be equally successful in a completely different cultural context in, say, China. Hofstede's work (2007) also contains another message for multinationals. He argues that countries, especially big

40 countries like China, India, Indonesia, and Brazil do not have a single national culture but many cultures that vary from region to region. A similar point could be made for smaller countries, in Western Europe for example, where different cultures may be based on
45 ethnic group rather than region.

C Research has shown major cultural differences between East and West that are important for Western business people trying to do business in the East. Psychologists have shown that Eastern and Western cultures can
50 vary significantly in terms of perception, logic, and how they see the world around them. Apparently, Western people focus more on detail while Eastern people tend to look at things as a whole. For example, when asked to look at a picture of a tiger in a forest, American
55 students focused on the tiger while Chinese students focused more on the background, i.e. the context the tiger was in.

D Researchers think this is caused by different social environments. In East Asia, social environments are
60 more complex, collective, and controlled. As a result, Eastern people need to pay attention to the social context if they are to operate effectively. On the other hand, Western societies prize individual freedom and there is not the same need to pay attention to the social
65 environment. Western people tend to view events as the result of specific people, while those raised in the East set the events in a broader context.

E Cultural differences influence the way firms in the East and West do business. For example, meetings in
70 North America or Europe have formal agendas setting the order in which items are discussed, and each item is resolved before moving to the next. The Japanese, rather than deal with agenda items in a fixed sequence, may prefer a more flexible approach which allows
75 them to get a better general idea. To Western people, meetings in Japan may appear unstructured, confused, and even threatening. However, Japanese managers are well used to such uncertainty.

F The result is that business has to take cultural
80 differences into account when considering entry to foreign markets through exports, joint ventures, or through takeovers. Similarities between the domestic and foreign cultural rules and values may make entry for a firm easier. Large differences may cause major
85 difficulties due to confusion and conflict where social groups do not want to give up valued elements of their culture (Oudenhoven and van der See 2002).

Source: L. Hamilton & P Webster, *The International Business Environment*, Oxford University Press, Oxford, 2009, pp151, 152, 154, 155

Business vocabulary

A | Understanding the function of vocabulary patterns

Vocabulary patterns can help you to identify the type of text you are reading, which helps you to understand the writer's aim.

1 Which paragraph in the text on page 25 contains a lot of noun + *of* + noun collocations?

2 What is the function of this paragraph? Tick (✓) the correct answer.

   a Comparative (considers similarities and differences)

   b Descriptive (defines and describes)

   c Evaluative (considers how good/important something is)

3 What do phrases a–c describe or refer to in the text?

   a a system of shared beliefs (line 1)

   _____

   b parts of culture (line 5/6)

   _____

   c the process of globalization (line 17)

   _____

B | Culture and the world

1 Replace the phrases in *italics* with these words and phrases.

   globalization migration   national   multinational
   regions   ethnic group exports

   a The Japanese economy relies a lot on *products sold to other countries.* _____

   b *Increasing trade between countries around the world* has made cultural differences smaller. _____

   c The company is *one that operates all around the world* so it has to consider cultural differences. _____

   d The problem is *one for the whole country* and needs to be addressed by the government. _____

   e Different *parts* of the country have different cultures. _____

   f They are a minority *racial population.* _____

   g *The movement of people from one place to another* has increased in recent years. _____

2 Choose three of the words from 2 to describe changes in your country in recent years.

   _____

   _____

   _____

   _____

   _____

   _____

3 Look at the text on page 25 and find collocations with *cultural* to complete the diagram.

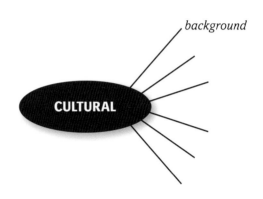

4 Complete the sentences with collocations from 3.

   a If a product fails in another country, companies often look for _____ as to why it happened.

   b Many _____ are unwritten because everyone in the culture understands them so well.

   c _____ can cause misunderstanding between people. For example, one gesture can have quite different meanings in different cultures.

   d My _____ has been influenced by my Italian mother and German father.

   e Something that is acceptable in the _____ of one country can be offensive in another.

5 What experiences have you had of other cultures? Use the collocations from 3 to describe differences you noticed or experienced.

Writing skills

| Concluding sentences

The concluding sentence usually performs one of three functions:

- summarizes the main idea of the paragraph
- draws logical conclusions based on the evidence presented
- links to the next paragraph

It often reminds the reader of the topic sentence and can be written like the topic sentence but in different words. If it is drawing a logical conclusion, then phrases such as *therefore*, *as a result*, etc. are commonly used.

1 Read the paragraph and identify:

   a the topic sentence   _____
   b the supporting sentences   _____
   c the concluding sentence   _____

   [1]Culture can be seen as a system of shared beliefs between members of a society. [2]However, it is not only the culture of different countries that can vary but that of different ethnic groups, age groups, companies, etc. within a country. [3]Two people from the same country but of very different ages and ethnic backgrounds could have widely differing views and experiences of life. [4]To state that all people from X country will behave in a particular way or hold a particular view is too simplistic. [5]Therefore, we need to carefully consider what is meant by the term *members of society*.

2 **Look back at the text on page 25. What is the function of the concluding sentence of each paragraph? Write *S* (summary), *C* (logical conclusion), or *L* (link).**

   A ___   D ___
   B ___   E ___
   C ___

3 **Rewrite these topic sentences as concluding sentences, making the same point in different words.**

   a There are a number of differences between culture in the East and West that can impact on business.

   Therefore, these cultural differences are significant for business and the way they operate.

   b Cultural differences influence the way Americans do business in Japan.

   _____

   c Businesses who consider cultural differences are likely to be more successful.

   _____

4 **Read paragraphs a–c. Identify if they present an argument or a description.**

   For an argument, write a concluding sentence which draws a logical conclusion.

   For a description, write a concluding sentence which summarizes the main idea.

   a English is today considered a global language. However, how can a language be defined as global? A global language is a language that has reached a particular status in a number of societies. According to Crystal, this status can be as a first language, a second language with an official status in education, law and the media, or a priority language in foreign language learning. English fulfils all these criteria.

   _____

   _____

   b Adapting to different cultural expectations of education is key to becoming a successful student. Methods of assessment and the role of a student can vary significantly between countries. For example, the education system of Uganda is largely based on the memorization of facts. However, in the UK, analysis, evaluation, and critical thinking are considered more important. This is not to say that one method is better than another, simply that the expectations are different.

   _____

   _____

   c Britain is facing a number of challenges today largely due to the economic problems of recent years. These problems include: a high level of unemployment, which is still rising; unequal distribution of wealth, which is at its highest level since the Second World War; and high levels of individual and government debt, with both at record levels. Finally, the government is about to increase taxes.

   _____

   _____

Research task

Research two businesses that have attempted to operate in a very different culture. If possible, find one that has been successful and one that has not. Draw a conclusion to explain their success or failure.

7 Job security

Study focus

1 Do you know anyone who has worked for the same company all their life?

2 Do you expect to work for many companies or one company?

3 In the UK, in the past, it was common to work for just one company all your working life. However, today, it is common to work for many companies. What is the situation in your country? If it has changed, as in the UK, why do you think it has changed?

Reading strategies

A | Identifying the main argument

1 Read the text from a business studies textbook. Which statement a–c completes this sentence to summarize the main argument?

The development of flexible business practices has led to …

a mainly opportunities for the workforce.

b mainly threats for the workforce.

c both threats and opportunities for the workforce.

2 Read the section on *threats*. Which sentence a–c summarizes the main argument?

a People are not worried about change.

b Change is the main reason why people feel threatened.

c People feel threatened by increased routine caused by technology.

3 Read the section on *opportunities*. Which sentence a–c summarizes the main argument?

a These opportunities are seen by all people.

b These are possible opportunities if people are willing to change.

c These are the opportunities most people have taken.

4 Look at the *evaluation*. Which sentence a–c summarizes the main argument?

a The flexible firm is mainly positive for companies but negative for employees.

b The flexible firm has both positives and negatives for employees.

c The flexible firm is positive for employees but negative for companies.

B | Identifying specific opinions

Complete the sentences to summarize the specific opinion of the writer on each topic.

1 Insecurity

Most people see flexible business practices as a threat. However, _____ .

2 Threats

Change at work used to be unusual, but today it _____ .

3 Redundancy

Redundancy is likely to cause people to _____ .

4 Lack of job security

Lack of job security is having a _____ impact on family life.

5 Constant training

Later in life, training is often seen as _____ and _____ .

6 New challenges

People willing to adapt will be _____ .

7 Increased self-reliance

People will need to take responsibility for _____ .

8 Diverse career paths

Careers may become more _____ .

9 Learning new skills

People may find their career more _____ if _____ .

C | Reacting to the text

Think about these questions.

- Do you see job insecurity as an opportunity or a threat?
- Rank the threats in the order they most worry you (1 = most, 5 = least).
- Rank the opportunities in the order they most appeal to you (1 = most, 5 = least).

Work in small groups and compare your answers.

Flexible operations

A flexible approach to operations enables a firm to respond rapidly to changes in its environment. The key idea is to reduce the size of the business's core, and increase the use of flexible, temporary contract
5 workers. One way to achieve this is to contract out work, often called outsourcing. Outsourcing is when a firm uses sources outside the business to do jobs that used to be done internally. Linked to this very closely is the American idea of downsizing. This means reducing
10 the size of the firm to make it more responsive to the market-place.

Insecurity

A growing concern with the policies used to achieve flexibility is the effect on the workforce. The changes caused by flexible business practices can result in
15 particular threats. However, they will also give new opportunities if workers are willing and able to take advantage of them.

Threats

Human beings naturally fear change. People are creatures of habit, who feel most at ease when they
20 have a comfortable routine. The workplace was felt by many to be a stable place. One of the features of a good job was generally thought to be a 'job for life'. As industry has changed, these accepted ideas have been challenged. In fact, it could be said that change will be
25 the only constant in a worker's career. This constant change brings with it several consequences:

Redundancy: Workers need to feel valued and needed. With many businesses downsizing, there is a greater chance of workers being made redundant.

30 *Lack of job security:* A lack of job security can be difficult for workers who saw the traditional pattern of a job for life with a particular company. How can a worker plan to buy a house if he or she can only rely on two or three years' work at a time? What about family life or the
35 schooling of children if one partner needs to move to a different location in search of new job opportunities?

Constant training: To find employment in a changing industrial scene, workers have to constantly upgrade their skills or learn new ones. Traditionally, training
40 and education has been seen as being for young people only. Training later in life can be seen as losing valuable time. Or it is often seen negatively, especially if training has no obvious practical use in the workplace. Constantly having to train may also lead to workers
45 feeling overworked.

Opportunities

New challenges: Constant change within industry means there will always be new openings and new challenges for workers. Some people are very happy with the constant challenge of facing the unknown. They will be
50 willing to adapt to the changing needs of society to take advantage of the opportunities.

Increased self-reliance: To operate effectively within a flexible workforce, workers need to develop skills in a range of areas. It is the individual's responsibility to do
55 this. By diversifying their skills, workers will be able to sell themselves to potential employers more effectively. They can start to take charge of their own future.

Diverse career paths: The new patterns of work may enable workers to follow career paths that previously were
60 almost impossible. They may be able to use their range of skills to follow career paths that change along with the opportunities available. It may become almost impossible for a worker to become trapped by routine, undertaking the same tasks day after day for many years.

65 *Learning new skills:* Increased flexibility means a much greater possibility that workers will have to update their own skills at regular intervals. If workers can exercise more self-control over the direction of their career, they may follow paths they find particularly
70 beneficial and interesting.

An evaluation

The flexible firm has many attractions for businesses, especially in difficult economic times. It is unlikely, however, that the full benefits could be felt unless society as a whole changes significantly. The country
75 needs to cope with, and to accept, regular periods of unemployment and retraining. Firms must question, however, whether the move to flexibility has gone too far. Recently an airline looking for cost savings put one-fifth of the cabin staff on a new, flexible contract with
80 30% less pay. What is the likely effect on absence, staff turnover and motivation? Many companies could find themselves understaffed. In the long term, a move back to secure career paths may be the best way to ensure a top quality workforce.

Source: I. Marcourse, B. Martin, M. Surridge & N. Wall, *Business Studies*, Hodder Arnold, 1999, pp 276–278

Business vocabulary

| Prefixes

A prefix is a letter or a group of letters added to the beginning of a word to change its meaning. Understanding the meaning of a prefix can help to understand the meaning of a word.

1 Complete each word with a prefix to match its definition. Use the words in **bold** to help with the meaning of the prefix.

> out   in   over   en   under   down   up   re

  a _____sourcing – when a firm contracts somebody **outside** the main company to complete a task

  b _____sizing – making a company smaller by **reducing** the number of workers

  c _____security – a feeling of **not enough** security

  d _____grade – **raise** the standard of something

  e _____able – to **give someone the ability** to do something

  f _____staffed – having **less** staff than you need

  g _____worked – having **too much** work to do

  h _____training – when people are trained **again** to do something new

2 Complete the sentences with the words from 1.

  a The _____ of the company was likely to involve the closure of at least three branches.

  b The decision to _____ the computer system caused a lot of disruption, but the system is much more efficient now.

  c The increase in salary will _____ her to buy a new car.

  d He was so dissatisfied with his job in the bank that he decided _____ as a lawyer was his only option.

  e The _____ of a number of call centres abroad has led to many customers being frustrated with the service the company provides.

  f The increase in unemployment was creating a feeling of _____ throughout society.

  g The new contract created so much extra work that everyone felt _____ .

  h Our department is _____ at the moment. We should have at least ten people, but there are only seven.

3 Complete the words in the sentences with the prefixes from 1.

  a My monthly _____goings are bigger than my income, so I have to put a lot on my credit card.

  b The report was _____complete as it lacked clear outcomes.

  c The manager tried to _____sure that people did not have too much work.

  d The company introduced a paper _____cycling scheme to help cut its impact on the environment.

  e The government did not provide enough money for the project. As a result, the scheme was _____funded and had to close down.

  f He had to accept a lower salary because they _____graded his position in the company.

  g After falling for five months, the share price saw an _____turn this week.

  h The company _____estimated my ability when they promoted me. I was unable to do the job properly.

4 Choose the correct option to complete the sentences.

  a The *outsourcing / outgoings* of all office functions caused a number of people to leave the company.

  b As a result of the recession, the company is *downgrading / downsizing* and cutting its workforce by 30%.

  c It was difficult to accept the *insecurity / incomplete* proposal as there wasn't enough information about funding.

  d We are going to spend €1 million on *upturning / upgrading* our security system.

  e Her degree *enabled / ensured* her to gain a good starting position in the firm.

  f *Understaffed / Underfunded* projects rarely succeed because they need more money to be completed well.

  g The lack of people meant everyone was *overworked / overestimated* all the time.

  h *Retraining / Recycling* has become more common as job security has become worse and people often have to apply for new jobs.

Writing skills

A | Generating ideas

Brainstorming is a good way of generating ideas for an essay question. When you brainstorm, you quickly think of ideas related to a topic and write them down (on your own or in groups). You can then organize these ideas and create a structure for your essay.

1 Read this essay question and brainstorm ideas with a partner.

Job insecurity has a negative effect on people and companies. Discuss.

2 Compare your ideas with this list.

people fear change

increased redundancy

routine is comfortable

retraining to get a new job

risk of losing job leads to *poor motivation*

constant training is demotivating

training is for 'young' people

insecurity in personal life

buying a house

having to retrain impacts on income

temporary contracts

family commitments

part-time work

B | Organizing ideas

A mind map is a diagram used to generate ideas or to organize ideas from a brainstorming session.

1 Look at the mind map below for the essay question in section A1.

  a What is the central word?

  b What are the three main ideas connected to the central word?

2 Add the ideas in *italics* from the list in section A2 to the mind map. Where would you put your own ideas from the brainstorming in section A1?

3 Look back at the section on *opportunities* in the text on page 29. In pairs, brainstorm ideas from the text on the topic of 'the opportunities provided by flexible working practices'. Add any ideas of your own.

4 Use your ideas in 3 to create a mind map.

5 Compare your mind map with another pair.

Research task

1 Research employment in your country or the sector you want to work in. Find out about things such as:

- outsourcing
- the length of time people work for one company
- the number of different companies people work for
- job security concerns

2 Organize your findings in a mind map.

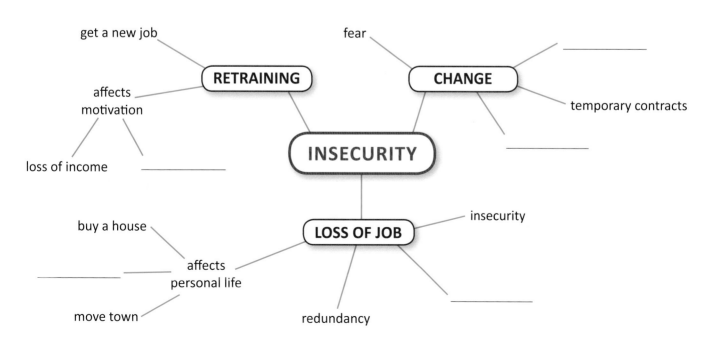

8 Sharing control

Study focus

1 In pairs, list five advantages of running your own company and five disadvantages.

2 Compare your lists with another pair.

Reading strategies

A | Scanning for specific information

1 Work in pairs. Read the text from a business magazine.

Student A Find one piece of information about:

Randall Bennett: _____

Eric Schmidt: _____

Phil Dur: _____

Peter Cobb: _____

Student B Find one piece of information about:

Robert Pickens: _____

Sheryl Sandberg: _____

Melinda Emerson: _____

Jon Nordmark: _____

2 Tell your partner what you found out about each person.

B | Reading closely for detailed information

1 Read the text again. Are the statements true or false for each paragraph? Circle *T* or *F*.

A Once people have shared control they see it as positive. T / F

B Bennett believes that sharing leadership will lead to growth. T / F

C The solution meant that Bennett could focus more time on day-to-day management of the business. T / F

D It is unusual to share leadership but easy to do. T / F

E Introducing new management needs to be done quickly and as soon as possible. T / F

F It is difficult for small companies to introduce new management. T / F

G You need to trust the new person and give them a clear role. T / F

H The future is important; the past is not. T / F

2 Correct the false statements in 1.

_____

_____

_____

_____

_____

3 Use your answers from 1 and 2 to summarize the main points the writer makes about sharing control.

_____

_____

_____

_____

C | Reacting to the text

1 Do you agree that sharing control is a 'delicate art'? Why or why not?

2 List three things you think would be positive and three things you think would be negative about sharing control of a company.

3 Compare your lists with a partner. What do your lists show about how you view control and working with others?

Expanding management: The delicate art of sharing control

A The thought of sharing control of your company can make people feel nervous. However, those who have done it think that having a second set of hands is fantastic. As long as they're the right hands.

B Since founding Secure Enterprise Computing in 1998, chairman Randall Bennett has seen business go up and down. But when the demand for security technology began to reach a peak a couple of years ago, he knew that he didn't want to miss the opportunity to grow
10 his company. He also knew that to benefit from the situation, he'd need to expand his leadership team and share control of the business. "You can have 100% of nothing or 50% of millions," Bennett says. "I've seen a lot of entrepreneurs fail over the years. They're not able
15 to give up [control]."

C The solution: employing Robert Pickens as president and chief operating officer of the Morrisville, N.C.-based firm last year. Pickens suggested a narrower strategic focus. He introduced quarterly reports and
20 measurements that give top managers an up-to-date picture of how the business is doing. With Pickens heading up operations, Bennett now has more time to develop new business and be the face of the company at community and industry meetings.

D Expanding the leadership team is a natural step when a company grows to be bigger than the skill set or capacity of its original founders. Google's Larry Page and Sergey Brin looked to Eric Schmidt when the time was right. Facebook's Mark Zuckerberg found Sheryl
30 Sandberg. It's a typical part of a start-up's growth path, but it's no easy task.

E Deciding what kind of person you want to add to the team is the most important step. The second is making the change carefully so that you get support from your
35 staff and any investors. Done right, the new team will bring energy and ideas into your business without weakening your core mission or changing the culture of the company. Phil Dur, managing director at Investor Growth Capital, recommends having lots of extended
40 meetings with any candidate, with vetting by the chief executive, senior managers, board members and any investors.

F At Secure Enterprise Computing, Pickens began as a consultant and won the respect of top executives as he
45 learned the business. It soon became clear that he was a good fit for the company. "It's difficult when you're a small company and you put someone in a management position because you need the rest of the group to respect and want that person in the new role," Bennett
50 says. "Sometimes people come in and think what they have to do is rock the boat. He [Pickens] spent a lot of time staying quiet, talking to everyone."

G After checking a new senior manager closely, it's important to give that person authority and autonomy,
55 advises Melinda Emerson, Philadelphia-based author of *Become Your Own Boss in 12 Months*. "You have to decide whether your ego can accept bringing another person in who's really making decisions that affect your business," Emerson says. "Not only do you have to have
60 clear roles for you and your new manager, but you have to make sure those roles are also clear to everyone at your company."

H It's also important to honor the history of the company and the qualities that built the business. Peter Cobb,
65 a co-founder of eBags, was impressed by Vince Jones when he took over as chief executive officer of the Denver-based retailer. Shortly after taking over, Jones organized a 10-year anniversary for eBags with a party at which the previous CEO, Jon Nordmark, gave a teary
70 speech about how proud he was to have Jones leading his company. "A lot of new CEOs would say, 'I don't want the ex-CEO within 100 miles of this place because people might prefer to support him,'" says Cobb, who was amazed at Jones's ability to balance appreciation
75 for the past with a need to kick the business into high gear. "For me as a founder, investor, shareholder, that's the best of both worlds."

Source: Katherine Reynolds Lewis, 'Expanding management: The delicate art of sharing control', *Fortune magazine*, 2011

Glossary

rock the boat (line 51): to cause problems and unrest
kick the business into high gear (line 75/76): to push the business forward quickly

Business vocabulary

A | Control

1 Match the words and phrases a–g from the text on page 33 to definitions 1–7.

   a share control (line 1) ____

   b second set of hands (line 3) ____

   c leadership team (line 11) ____

   d give up control (line 15) ____

   e head up (line 22) ____

   f authority (line 54) ____

   g autonomy (line 54) ____

   1 the ability to act and make decisions yourself without being controlled by others

   2 another person to share the workload with

   3 to no longer be in charge of someone or something

   4 a group of individuals that work together to run or manage a group or a project

   5 the power to give orders to people

   6 to be in charge of someone or something

   7 to divide power between people

2 Complete the text with the words and phrases from 1.

Some people prefer not to ¹_____ of a business with other people. However, a ²_____ to help with the workload can actually be very beneficial. And if a company wants to grow, it is often essential to increase the size of the ³_____ and share the running of the business. Each new manager can have a clear role and ⁴_____ a specific part of the company. An existing manager may at first be unwilling to ⁵_____ as they have played a key role in the development of the business. Also, they may have had a lot of ⁶_____ and be used to giving orders rather than working together with people. However, once they are able to share control and give ⁷_____ to the new members of the management team, it can be very positive for the whole company.

3 Work in pairs. Use the words and phrases from this section to talk about your views on control in the workplace.

B | Developing a business

1 Complete the table with these words and phrases. One phrase can go in more than one box.

build the business   found   reach a peak   grow
expand   develop   growth plan   co-founder

The start of a business	
The development of a business	
The time when a business is most successful	

2 Replace the words in *italics* with the words and phrases from 1. Change the form if necessary.

   a He was one of the *people responsible for the start* of the business. _____

   b Sales started to *get to their highest level* towards the end of 2008. _____

   c The long-term aim was to *make* their retail operations *bigger* by opening three more stores. _____

   d She wants to *improve* her skill set in order to have more job opportunities. _____

   e After *starting* the business in 2000, the company went on to become one of the largest in the world by 2010. _____

   f The company had an ambitious *aim to become bigger*. They wanted to increase their market share by 30% in five years. _____

   g Their plan was to *increase the size of* the business by taking on ten new employees and raising production by 20%. _____

   h They *created the company* from nothing. _____

3 Work in pairs. Use the words and phrases from 1 to talk about this company.

H. William started business 1995 with J. Maynard

<u>*Sales*</u>

2000 €1m   2010 €3m   2012 €2.7m

<u>*2013 Growth plan*</u>

increase staffing 15% + production 20%

open new stores in New York + Hong Kong

Writing skills

A | Taking notes from a text

It is usually not necessary, or even useful, to note down everything exactly when reading a text. You will be more interested in the main points or anything that is relevant to your studies. Taking notes efficiently will save you time.

1 Compare these notes with paragraph B in the text on page 33.

> *Bennett fnd Secure Enterprise Computing 1998*
> *Business ↑ ↓*
> *Demand for sec. tech. = peak means not miss*
>   *opportunity = expand lead. team*
> *100% nothing or 50% millions*
> *not give up cont. = entrepreneurs fail*

2 The notes in 1 contain several common techniques:

   a using abbreviations
   b using symbols
   c using content words
   d simplifying complex sentences

   <u>Underline</u> at least two examples of each technique in the notes.

3 Write suitable abbreviations for these commonly occurring words in the text.

   a found *fnd*
   b business _____
   c company _____
   d important _____
   e investor _____

4 In pairs, discuss what you think these symbols mean.

   a >
   b £
   c ≠
   d #

5 Look at paragraph C in the text on page 33.

   a Circle key content words. What do you notice about these words? Are they nouns, verbs, etc.?
   b Which complex sentences do you think could be simplified?
   c Compare your answers with a partner.

6 Work in pairs.

   Student A Write notes for paragraphs E and F. Focus on abbreviations, key content words and simplifying complex sentences.

   Student B Write notes for paragraphs G and H. Focus on abbreviations, key content words and simplifying complex sentences.

7 Give a spoken summary of your two paragraphs to your partner.

B | Expanding notes

You will need to expand your notes to use them in academic writing. Changing your notes into full sentences will mean that the ideas will be expressed in your own style of writing rather than the style of the original.

1 Look at the notes and the full sentence expanded from the notes.

> *Exp Leadsp = natural when comp bigger than founder's skills*

   Expanding leadership is natural when a company becomes bigger than the founder's skills.

2 Compare the sentence with the original sentence in paragraph D in the text (lines 25–27).

   a Is the meaning the same?
   b Is the structure the same?
   c Is the idea expressed in original language?

3 Look at the notes on paragraph B again. Expand each part into a full sentence, e.g.:

> *Bennett fnd Secure Enterprise Computing 1998*
> *Secure Enterprise Computing was founded by Bennett in 1998.*

4 Look at your notes from another paragraph.

   a Expand your notes to form full sentences.
   b Compare your sentence to the original text. Have you kept the same meaning? Have you expressed the idea originally?

Research task

Many people talk positively about Google's leadership style. Research the history of Google's leadership and find out what is particularly unique in its leadership style.

Study focus

1 In pairs, brainstorm a list of different departments in a company, e.g. Marketing.

2 Still in pairs, rank these departments in order of importance to the success of a company (1 = most important, 5 = least important).

Marketing   Finance   Human Resources
Operations Management   Research & Development

3 Discuss your ranking with another pair. Explain your choices.

Reading strategies

A | Reading quickly for main ideas

1 Read the text from a business studies textbook. Which statement a–c completes this summary of the text best?

Operations management is …
a of less use to business today.
b of growing importance in a globalized world.
c able to solve most problems a business faces.

2 Match summaries 1–4 to the four main sections of the text a–d.

a Introduction ____
b What is operations management? ____
c How important is operations management for international competitiveness? ____
d When does a fad become a trend? ____

1 Operations Management deals with issues such as location, efficiency, innovation, stock control, quality control and organization.

2 Some people believe in the Japanese idea of 'continuous improvement'; others think the idea is of no benefit to businesses.

3 A number of departments claim to be the most important in a company. Operations Management could also make this claim.

4 Quality and cost are key to success in an international market.

B | Identifying the writer's point of view

Read the text again. Choose the correct statement to complete the writer's point of view.

1 Operations Management is …
a more important than the Marketing and Personnel Departments.
b less important than the Marketing and Personnel Departments.
c of equal importance to the Marketing and Personnel departments.

2 Production methods are changed to …
a improve market research methods.
b make staff feel more motivated and increase production.
c help control stock levels.

3 To compete internationally, a company …
a needs a good marketing strategy.
b needs to pay attention to the exchange rate.
c needs to focus on price and standard of products.

4 Developments in operations management can …
a solve all problems a business faces.
b apply to any situation without need for change.
c work in any situation if they are adapted well.

C | Reacting to the text

Look at these questions related to operations management. In pairs, discuss which questions you think are most important and why. Which issues will be more important for service firms? Which will be more important for production firms?

• Where should the firm be located?
• How can the firm develop more innovative products and services?
• How can the firm become more efficient?
• How can the firm control its quality?
• How best can the firm control its stock?
• How best can the workforce be organized?

Operations management – an overview

Introduction

All departments in an organisation like to see themselves as the most important. Marketing people argue that without successful marketing even the greatest product in the world would fail. Those who
5 work in personnel argue that without motivation, marketing and sales staff would achieve little.

Operations management can also claim a position of importance in the same way. Mercedes cars, Sony electronics and Boeing airplanes are not just
10 well packaged. They are brilliantly conceived and developed, and superbly made. They are wonderful examples of the potential of top-class operations management.

These days the importance of productive efficiency
15 is widely recognised. The globalisation of business means that firms have to compete internationally. How do they do this? Through the adoption of production techniques and ideas which set standards (benchmarking) and then make the best possible use
20 of resources (lean production) to produce the best possible products (R&D, efficiency).

What is operations management?

Operations management is seen most easily in the management of the production process, but it covers a much wider range of ideas. In particular, the phrase
25 is used equally for both firms who provide a service and those involved in production. The same sorts of questions need to be answered, such as:
- Where should the firm be located?
- How can the firm develop more innovative products
30   and services?
- How can the firm become more efficient?
- How can the firm control its quality?
- How best can the firm control its stock?
- How best can the workforce be organised?

35 The management of operations is closely linked to the management of people. The main reason for changing production methods is to improve motivation and productivity. In a similar way, the design and development function of operations management must
40 be connected to the results of market research and the firm's competitive position.

When considering operations management it is also important to understand the following underlying issues.

Issue 1 How important is operations management for international competitiveness?

A major reason for the growing importance of
45 operations management is the need for firms to compete more effectively on an international stage.

The start of the Euro on 1 January 1999 was one of the European developments that forced firms such as Tesco and Kingfisher to look beyond Britain. And
50 it is not only about UK firms looking to Europe. The 'shrinking' of the world through the improvements in transport and communications have made many British firms develop a more international perspective.

All areas of business need to be effective for a
55 company to compete internationally. But the most important areas are the cost and quality of products. A company needs to produce the best quality products at competitive costs to succeed in the international market. However, getting everything right internally is
60 still not a guarantee of success. External factors such as high exchange rates can damage the competitiveness of the most efficient firms.

Issue 2 When does a fad become a trend?

The 'Japanisation' of UK businesses has become widely established in recent years. The idea of kaizen (a focus
65 on continuous improvement of processes), quality circle groups and aiming for zero defects are now common in both business literature and the workplace. There are, however, people who feel that these ideas are either:
- ideas that are already known about, or
70 - broad generalisations with little connection to the real world.

They argue that these ideas are more for the benefit of business 'gurus' who can earn a lot of money selling books based on these 'new' ideas than for the benefit
75 and development of businesses. For evidence, they can point to many examples of businesses that have applied these ideas but shown no improvement or have even gone into further decline.

It is important to realise that the newer developments
80 in operations management are no miracle cure for businesses. There is no one solution that will raise every business to levels of international competitiveness. The real task for managers is to adapt the principles and culture to their own individual
85 situation, and continue adapting them over time as that situation changes.

Source: I. Marcourse, B. Martin, M. Surridge & N. Wall, *Business Studies*, Hodder Arnold, 1999, pp 412–413

Glossary

conceive (line 10): plan or imagine
fad (Heading: Issue 2): style or activity that is very popular for a short period of time

Business vocabulary

| Competition, status and success

1 Replace the words and phrases in *italics* with these words and phrases.

> achieve   widely recognized   set standards
> compete effectively   win a share   widely established

a This product is *commonly thought of* as the best of its kind. _____

b It was difficult for the company to *gain a part* of the European soft drinks market.
_____

c The company's production techniques *established levels of quality* that all other companies wanted to copy. _____

d After much hard work, he was able *to succeed in meeting* the production targets set by his line manager. _____

e After launching in 1990, the company is now *in a well-respected position because of its success* in its field.
_____

f The changes in the management system meant that the company was able to *succeed in being better than other companies* in the market.
_____

2 Use the words and phrases from 1 to write a sentence about each of the following.

a a company that is widely established in its sector

   Apple is widely established as a market leader in computing.

b something you have recently achieved

   _____

   _____

c a change a company could make to compete more effectively

   _____

   _____

d a product that is widely recognized in a particular market

   _____

   _____

e a country in which companies are trying to win a share of the market

_____

_____

f who you think should be responsible for setting standards in a company

_____

_____

3 Find words or phrases in the text on page 37 to match definitions a–f. Some letters have been given to help.

a the possibility to have success in the future (lines 7–13)

   p _ _ _ nt _ _ l

b a firm's place in the market in relation to other companies (lines 35–41)

   c _ _ _ et _ _ _ _ e   p _ _ _ _ i _ n

c something that makes doing well certain to happen (lines 54–62)

   g _ _ _ an _ _ e   _ f   s _ _ c _ _ s

d to always get better (lines 63–71)

   c _ _ _ in _ _ _ s   im _ _ _ _ e _ _ _ t

e an advantage (lines 72–78)

   b _ _ _ _ _ t

f the ability to participate and try to win (lines 79–86)

   c _ _ p _ _ _ _ iv _ _ _ ss

4 Complete the sentences with the words and phrases from 3.

a Investing large amounts of money is not a _____ – a business can still fail.

b Despite having a lot of _____ , he failed to reach a high level in the organization.

c The _____ of the media sector causes a lot of people to leave and look for a job with less stress and competition.

d His work got better and better and he showed _____ throughout his career.

e The main _____ to the company of the recent charity event was a more positive reputation in the media.

f The company's _____ improved when it merged and it became the market leader.

Writing skills

An effective introduction should clearly set out the aims of the piece of writing. A reader should not need to know the essay question to understand your aims. Introductions follow many patterns depending on essay length, subject area and the type of essay question. However, there are some features common to most introductions.

A | Writing an effective introduction

1 Read this introduction and answer questions a–d.

Many people put the success of Mercedes down to the design and engineering of its products. Whilst this is a key factor in its success, a number of other factors impact on the company's ability to achieve its aims and objectives. Strategic decisions such as what to produce, where and when are equally key to the quality of what is produced. This essay will argue that without successful operations management a company may fail no matter how good its product is. Firstly, this essay will look at factors affecting success and then evaluate the relative importance of each of these.

a What do you think the topic of the essay is?

_____

_____

b What could be the question or title of the essay?

_____

_____

c What main points do you think will be in the essay?

_____

_____

d What is the reason for writing?

_____

_____

2 Look at the four main features of introductions a–d. Underline these features in the introduction in 1.

a interesting the reader by using a quotation, a question, an interesting fact, a definition or general background information
b more specific information on the essay's topic
c a thesis statement – showing the main argument or point of view
d an indication of the essay's structure

3 Read the essay question. Put sentences a–e into the correct order to form a logical introduction.

The management of operations is closely linked to the management of people. Discuss.

a Firstly, this essay will look at a number of management systems. It will then look at how these systems can be applied equally to both people and organizations. ____

b However, mechanization changed many people's perspectives of individual roles in the workplace. ____

c In the past, people were seen very much as part of the production process and no different from any other tool used in production. ____

d This essay will argue that people can be managed in the same way as a system is managed even if a slightly more personal touch is needed. ____

e Whilst the roles of individuals have changed, this does not mean to say that the methods of management have changed vastly. ____

4 Compare your answer with a partner.

B | Writing practice

1 Write an introduction to one of these two essay questions. Use the text to help with ideas.

a Operations management can be used equally in both the production and the service industry. Discuss.

b Globalization has increased the importance of operations management. Discuss.

2 Exchange your introduction with a partner. Check your partner has included each of the main features from section A2.

Research task

Business 'gurus' are accused of writing about things that are already known. Find a book by a well-known business guru and look at its main ideas. To what extent would you say the accusation is true for this guru?

Study focus

1 Have you ever worked in an office? If so, describe your office to a partner. Think about the space, your desk, meeting rooms, etc.

2 List two advantages and two disadvantages of each of these types of office.

individual office   open plan office

3 Compare your lists with a partner.

Reading strategies

A | Understanding a text using background knowledge

1 You are going to read a text from a business magazine. Look at the title of the text. In pairs, make three predictions about what the future workplace might look like.

2 Compare and discuss your predictions with another pair.

3 What do you know about these things? How might they have changed the working environment?

a Blackberries

_____

b flexible working space

_____

c virtual working environment

_____

d hybrid workspaces

_____

e face-to-face communication

_____

4 Read the text quickly. How similar are your ideas in 1 and 3 to those in the text?

B | Identifying arguments for and against

Read the text again and answer the questions for each paragraph.

A What two advantages of combining a physical and virtual working environment does the writer present?

B Does the writer present arguments for or against the increased use of technology? What are these arguments?

C What argument against open office spaces does the writer present?

D What arguments does the writer present in favour of the hybrid working environment?

E How does this paragraph support the arguments presented in paragraph D?

F What does the writer identify as the main challenge arising from changes to ways of working?

G What argument does the writer present against entirely virtual working environments?

C | Reacting to the text

1 Which of these environments would you prefer to work in? Rank in order from 1 (the most) to 3 (the least).

traditional closed office space   _____

entirely virtual environment   _____

hybrid working environment   _____

2 Compare your ranking with a partner. Explain your choices.

3 Discuss in pairs. Would the working environments in 1 be more suitable for some jobs than others? Which environment would suit each of these jobs and why?

accountant

marketing executive

key account manager

R&D worker

senior manager

What will the future workplace look like?

Businesses can capitalize on the evolving nature of the office by striking a balance that combines virtual and physical work space.

A Unless you have been on vacation for the past few years, you are probably aware that the workplace as we know it is rapidly changing. The 9-to-5 routine spent in an "official" office is giving way to the virtual work environment; the at-my-desk-by-8:59 is becoming the on-my-Blackberry 24/7, and the Starbucks coffee break has become the Starbucks "home" office. This isn't necessarily a bad thing. Businesses can capitalize on the evolving nature of the office by striking a balance that combines virtual and physical work and space. This could eventually increase productivity and lower costs without giving up company culture or individual motivation.

B Information technology has changed the ideas of where work happens and the role of buildings. Innovative corporate leaders have already recognized that technology allows their employees to be mobile, to work with colleagues remotely and across time zones, and to get work done in a variety of settings both inside and outside of the traditional office. These businesses have saved money, increased work flexibility, and made the best use of their real estate. And these new flexible workplaces are also providing gains in worker productivity.

C Today, companies are increasingly focusing on the problem of how to help employees concentrate and get work done (which is traditionally thought to require an enclosed office space) while also allowing for the significant benefits of open and flexible office environments, including creativity, knowledge, teamwork and coordination. We know that open environments can slow down work. We also know that they can promote interaction and knowledge sharing.

D So what is the solution? Enter the hybrid workplace. Hybrid environments provide a mix of enclosed and open work spaces that are available for users to occupy on an as-needed basis. The mobility we now have allows individuals to choose how and where they work best. A flexible work environment can balance the needs for individual work with the need for interaction. The arrival of mobile technology and mobile ways of using space means that companies don't really need to decide between openness versus enclosure when designing a workplace. Hybrid work spaces offer both open and closed environments that can be useful in a variety of ways. In a hybrid workplace, employees have the option of working individually in a quiet space or working with their colleagues in open, collaborative team areas or rooms. Furthermore, the hybrid workplace can take advantage of technology to combine face-to-face and virtual collaboration – both within the office and remotely.

E Cisco's McCarthy Ranch campus in Milpitas, California has become a hybrid workplace. Hundreds of mobile workers who use the campus have access to eight different kinds of unassigned work spaces: workstations, touchdown spaces, privacy rooms, focus booths, open project spaces, team rooms, lounges and dens. The spaces support many different kinds of virtual collaboration using IP technology and audio and video conferencing. And Cisco isn't alone. As reported in the *New York Times*, companies like Intel and Deloitte are using similar strategies to make the office space they have more flexible.

F What is on the horizon for the workplace? It's fair to expect the following:
- Continuous change in the way workers collaborate by using new technology
- New cultural norms and protocols for virtual working
- More opportunities to plan for shared work spaces with outside organizations
- Demands for cities and city governments to create space to support new ways of working

All of these changes will present challenges to the way in which workplaces are designed and built by developers, architects, landlords and suppliers of all kinds.

G The idea that virtual communication and remote work environments will entirely replace the need to physically gather people together is perhaps not true. Face-to-face communication allows for fast paced and unplanned interactions, which help to speed up decision making and information flow in ways that have not yet been fully matched by virtual work environments. At the same time, traditional work environments are becoming increasingly unproductive and will soon be outdated among the leading corporations, if they aren't already. The hybrid workplace is the future and will be essential for businesses looking to stay ahead.

Source: Andrew Laing, 'What will the future workplace look like?', *Fortune magazine*, 2011

Glossary

strike a balance (line 12): to find an acceptable position which is between two things
real estate (line 24): buildings or land
on the horizon (line 67): in the near future

Business vocabulary

A | Pronoun referencing

Pronouns are often used to refer to something earlier in a text. They help to avoid the repetition of key words and phrases, but sometimes this makes the text harder to follow. The reader has to work out which noun the pronoun is referring to. Recognizing pronoun referencing will help you to connect ideas and information in a text.

1 **Look at this sentence from the text on page 41. The underlined pronoun refers to the highlighted word.**

   Unless you have been on vacation for the past few years, you are probably aware that the workplace as we know it is rapidly changing.

2 **Underline the pronouns in these sentences from the text. Circle the ideas they refer to.**

   a Businesses can capitalize on the evolving nature of the office by striking a balance that combines virtual and physical work and space. This could eventually increase productivity and lower costs without giving up company culture or individual motivation.

   b We know that open environments can slow down work. We also know that they can promote interaction and knowledge sharing.

   c The mobility we now have allows individuals to choose how and where they work best.

3 **Read the text and answer the questions below.**

   The workplace has changed significantly in recent years. ¹It is no longer one fixed location. ²This is largely possible due to major developments in the technology used in the workplace. ³These include the ability to teleconference, to email on the move and to store much work data on portable devices. Each of ⁴_____ developments has decreased the need for a fixed working space. The long-term impact of ⁵_____ change is not fully clear. However, ⁶_____ is likely that the traditional office space will become less and less important.

   a What does each pronoun 1–3 refer to?

      1 _____

      2 _____

      3 _____

   b Which is the correct pronoun for 4–6?

      this   these   it

B | Change

1 **Match phrases a–d from the text on page 41 to definitions 1–4.**

   a rapidly changing (line 6)   ____
   b evolving nature (line 12)   ____
   c increase productivity (line 14)   ____
   d lower costs (line 14)   ____

   1 a change that means more of something is happening
   2 a change happening quickly
   3 a change happening gradually over a period of time
   4 a change that means less of something

2 *Increase* **is both a verb and a noun. Underline the verb and circle the noun in these sentences.**

   a There was a 20% increase in profits during last year.
   b Profits increase by 20% year on year.

3 **What is the verb for each of these nouns?**

   a rise   _____   e decline   _____
   b increase   _____   f reduction   _____
   c fluctuation _____   g fall   _____
   d decrease   _____   h drop   _____

4 **Complete the table with these words.**

   | minimal | sudden | slight | gradual | rapid | sharp |
   | steep | steady | marked | dramatic |

small or slow change	
quick or large change	

5 **Complete the sentences with words from 4 to show the type of change being described.**

   a There was a *sudden* rise in the share price of 20% in just one day.
   b There was a _____ increase in the share price of 20% over a four-year period.
   c There has been a _____ fluctuation in the price of the last week as it has remained around the £5 mark.
   d There has been a _____ decline in the price from £4 to £3.50 over a two-year period.
   e Many retailers have introduced a _____ reduction in price, cutting prices by as much as 40%.

Writing skills

A | Structuring a paragraph

A paragraph is a group of related sentences that develops a writer's topic. It usually follows a standard structure that includes a topic sentence, supporting ideas and concluding ideas. It can also include sentences to transition between paragraphs.

1 Read this paragraph from the text on page 41 and identify parts a–d.

[1]Information technology has changed the ideas of where work happens and the role of buildings. [2]Innovative corporate leaders have already recognized that technology allows their employees to be mobile, to work with colleagues remotely and across time zones, and to get work done in a variety of settings both inside and outside of the traditional office. [3]These businesses have saved money, increased work flexibility, and made the best use of their real estate. [4]And these new flexible workplaces are also providing gains in worker productivity.

  a concluding sentence ____

  b short explanation to support the main idea ____

  c topic sentence giving the main idea ____

  d identification of the results/implications of the main idea ____

2 Put the sentences into a logical order to make a paragraph.

  a Hundreds of mobile workers who use the campus have access to eight different kinds of unassigned work spaces: workstations, touchdown spaces, privacy rooms, focus booths, open project spaces, team rooms, lounges and dens. ____

  b Cisco's McCarthy Ranch campus in Milpitas, California has gone the way of the hybrid workplace. ____

  c The spaces support many different kinds of virtual collaboration using IP technology and audio and video conferencing. ____

  d And Cisco is far from alone. As reported in the *New York Times*, companies like Intel and Deloitte are using similar strategies to make the office space they have more flexible. ____

3 Check your order against paragraph D in the text on page 41.

B | Writing practice

1 Work in pairs, Student A and Student B. Read your topic sentence below. Develop this sentence to make a paragraph containing at least three more sentences – two to support the main idea and one to conclude the paragraph.

Student A

Companies can gain significant benefits by encouraging innovative uses of space.

Student B

A solely virtual work environment has a number of disadvantages.

_____

_____

_____

_____

_____

_____

_____

_____

2 Check your partner's paragraph. Does it:

• have logical explanations or examples?

• have a relevant concluding sentence?

3 Work in pairs.

  a Each student writes a topic sentence related to an innovative product.

  b Give your topic sentence to your partner. Check you understand the main idea of the sentence.

  c Develop your partner's topic sentence into a full paragraph.

  d Exchange paragraphs again. Check each other's paragraph for organization.

Research task

Find out what these expressions mean in terms of work environments. How would you feel about working in each of these environments?

hot-desking   telecommuting

Decision making

Study focus

1 Write down:

a good decision you made

a bad decision you made

2 **Show your decisions to a partner then discuss these questions.**

a Do you think the good decision was lucky or carefully planned?

b How could your bad decision have been made better?

Reading strategies

A | Identifying main ideas

Read the text from an academic textbook about marketing and answer the questions.

1 What is the aim of Vroom and Yetton's decision-making model? (para. A)

2 How many leadership styles are there? What are they? (para. B)

3 Do Vroom and Yetton believe that one style is better than another? (para. C)

4 How many characteristics of problems are there? (para. D)

5 What is it important for managers to be? (para. E)

6 How is the model used? (para. F)

B | Identifying supporting detail

Read the text again and answer the questions.

1 The model aims to influence the quality and acceptability of decisions. How is this achieved? (para. A)

2 When is it not worth consulting subordinates? (para. C)

3 Why is it important for a manager to be able to adapt? (para. E)

4 Why is the model used in management training? (para. F)

C | Understanding the relationship between text and graphic

Look at the figure in the text and answer the questions.

1 Which two paragraphs relate mainly to the figure?

2 Where are the leadership styles shown on the figure?

3 Where are the problem criteria shown on the figure?

4 How many times is the autocratic leadership style considered the most effective?

5 How many times is the negotiating leadership style considered the most effective?

6 Do you think the figure shows that one decision-making style is better than another? Does the text state that one is better than another?

7 Briefly summarize the main idea of the figure.

_____

_____

_____

_____

D | Reacting to the text

1 **Do you agree that none of the five leadership styles is better than the others?**

2 **Rank the leadership styles in order from the one you think would be most like you to the one that would be least like you.**

AI (Autocratic) ____

AII (Information seeking) ____

CI (Consulting) ____

CII (Negotiating) ____

G (Group) ____

3 **Compare your ranking with a partner and discuss the questions.**

a What situations do you think your partner might find most difficult to lead in?

b Do you think your partner's leadership style would make them better at working in a particular environment?

Vroom and Yetton's decision model

A The idea behind Vroom and Yetton's (1973) contingency model of decision making is to influence the quality and acceptability of decisions. This depends on the manager choosing how best to involve subordinates in making a decision – and being willing to
5 change their style to match the situation. The model defines five leadership styles and seven characteristics of problems. Managers can use these characteristics to diagnose the situation. They can find the recommended way of reaching a decision on that problem by using the decision tree shown in Figure 1.

B The five leadership styles defined are:
1 *AI (Autocratic)* You solve the problem or make the decision yourself using information available to you at that time.
2 *AII (Information seeking)* You obtain the necessary information from your subordinate(s), then decide on the solution to the
15 problem yourself. You may or may not tell your subordinates what the problem is in getting the information from them. The role played by your subordinates in making the decision is clearly one of providing the necessary information to you rather than generating or evaluating alternative solutions.
20 3 *CI (Consulting)* You share the problem with relevant subordinates individually, getting their ideas and suggestions without bringing them together as a group. Then you make the decision that may or may not reflect your subordinates' influence.

4 *CII (Negotiating)* You share the problem
25 with your subordinates as a group, obtaining their collective ideas and suggestions. Then you make the decision that may or may not reflect your subordinates' influence.

30 5 *G (Group)* You share the problem with your subordinates as a group. Together you generate and evaluate alternatives and attempt to reach agreement (consensus) on a solution. Your role is much like
35 that of a chairperson. You do not try to influence the group to adopt 'your' solution, and you are willing to accept and implement any solution that has the support of the entire group.

C The idea behind the model is that no style is in itself better than another. Some believe that consultative or delegating styles are naturally preferable to autocratic approaches because they are more in
45 keeping with democratic principles. Vroom and Yetton argue otherwise. In some situations (such as when time is short or the manager has all the information needed for a minor decision) going through the process
50 of consultation will waste time and add little value. In other situations, such as where the subordinates have the relevant information, it is essential to consult them. The point of the model is to make managers more aware
55 of the range of factors to take into account in using a particular decision-making style.

D The problem criteria are expressed in seven diagnostic questions:
1 Is one solution likely to be better than
60 another?
2 Does the manager have enough information to make a high-quality decision?
3 Is the problem structured?
65 4 Is acceptance of the decision by subordinates critical to effective implementation?
5 If the manager makes the decision alone, is it likely to be accepted by subordinates?
70 6 Do subordinates share organisational goals?
7 Is conflict likely amongst subordinates over preferred solutions?

E The Vroom–Yetton decision model implies
75 that managers need to be flexible in the style they adopt. The style should be appropriate to the situation rather than

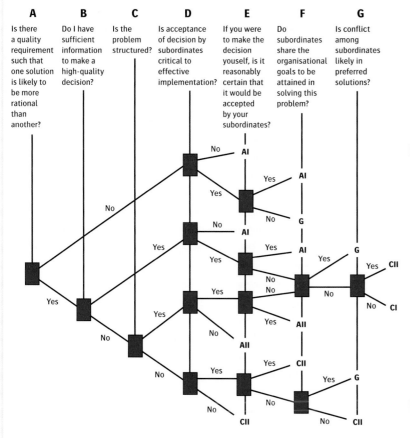

A	B	C	D	E	F	G
Is there a quality requirement such that one solution is likely to be more rational than another?	Do I have sufficient information to make a high-quality decision?	Is the problem structured?	Is acceptance of decision by subordinates critical to effective implementation?	If you were to make the decision youself, is it reasonably certain that it would be accepted by your subordinates?	Do subordinates share the organisational goals to be attained in solving this problem?	Is conflict among subordinates likely in preferred solutions?

Figure 1: Vroom and Yetton's decision tree

consistent amongst all situations. The problem with this is that managers may find it difficult to switch
80 between styles, perhaps several times a day. Although the approach appears objective, it still depends on the manager answering the questions. Requiring a simple yes or no answer to complex questions is too simple, and managers often want to say 'it all depends' on
85 other historical or contextual factors.

F Nevertheless the model is used in management training to alert managers to the style they prefer to use and to the range of options available. It also prompts managers to consider systematically whether that

90 preferred style is always appropriate. They may then handle situations in a more planned way than if they relied only on their preferred style or intuition.

Source: P. Baines, C. Fill & K. Page, *Marketing*, Oxford University Press, Oxford, 2008, pp229–231

Glossary

subordinate (line 25): a person less important than you in an organization

Business vocabulary

A | Word formation

1 **The text contains several words formed from verbs a–e. Match the verbs to definitions 1–5.**

   a accept ___   c evaluate ___   e prefer ___
   b consult ___   d implement ___

   1 to like something better than another thing
   2 to discuss something with another person before you decide something
   3 to think carefully about something before you judge how good or useful it is
   4 to agree to or approve of something
   5 to make an idea, plan start to happen

2 **What other forms of each verb do you know? Make a list under these headings.**

   Noun   Adjective   Adverb

3 **Compare your lists in pairs then check which forms are in the text. Add any extra forms to your list.**

4 **Complete the sentences with the correct form of the words in brackets.**

   a The outcome of the decision was not _____ (accept) to most people.
   b After much _____ (consult), it was decided to move ahead with the project.
   c They decided to _____ (evaluate) all the possible alternatives.
   d The _____ (implement) of the plan was more difficult than people imagined.
   e We need to make a decision this week, _____ (prefer) before Friday.

B | Leadership and decision making

1 **Choose the correct option to complete the sentences.**

   a He is very *autocratic / democratic* in his leadership style and rarely involves others in the decision-making process.
   b She likes to *delegate / evaluate* boring office tasks to her colleagues wherever possible.
   c He likes to *negotiate / implement* solutions to problems with his employees and reach an agreement that everyone is happy with.
   d She likes to *consult / accept* employees during the decision-making process so she can hear their ideas and suggestions.
   e The *criteria / goals* used to judge the success of the project were written by the consultancy firm.
   f The manager ensured that her *objectives / subordinates* were very clear about their roles in the team.

2 **Replace each word or phrase in *italics* with one of the words not used in 1.**

   a The firm's main *aims* were to increase productivity and cut production costs by 10%. _____
   b The company director believes that the decision-making process should be *with equal participation by all* and therefore he seeks the views of all employees. _____
   c The company *judge* people on current performance not past success. _____
   d Once they decided to *put* the plan *into action,* it quickly became a success. _____
   e The company found it very easy to *say yes to* the employees' requests as they were very reasonable. _____

3 **What do you think is the best way for managers to make decisions? Write three sentences using words from 1 and 2.**

Writing skills

A | Writing a conclusion

The conclusion of a piece of academic writing usually has two parts.

The first part summarizes the main ideas and restates the thesis statement from the introduction.

The second part gives your final comments and may include logical conclusions based on the evidence presented, predictions and your closing thoughts on the topic.

The conclusion should not include any new ideas or information.

1 **Which sentence in the concluding paragraph below restates this thesis statement?**

This essay will argue that there is little empirical support to show that one decision-making method is better than another.

[1]In conclusion, managers can make decisions using a number of methods. [2]Although some would argue that some decision-making methods are clearly better than others, there is little evidence to show that this is the case. [3]As Vroom and Yetton's model shows, it is more appropriate for managers to adopt different decision-making strategies depending on the context. [4]Whilst it may be possible for a perfect decision-making model to be developed, it is unlikely given the variety of individuals and contexts involved in such processes.

2 **What is the function of the other sentences in the concluding paragraph? Write the sentence number.**

  a logical conclusion   ____

  b summary of main ideas   ____

  c closing thoughts   ____

3 **Match thesis statements a–c to paraphrased versions 1–3 used in a conclusion.**

  a This model, whilst perhaps ideal, is not realistic in a practical situation when time is short and the manager already has any relevant information. ____

  b Decisions do not follow a logical pattern and good decisions are often made more by luck than judgement. ____

  c Whilst consultative methods of management are more popular today, it can be argued that autocratic leadership is more appropriate in a number of situations such as where the work involves everyday tasks with few problems to solve. ____

1 Due to a lack of information or understanding of information, it is therefore likely that good decisions happen by chance rather than rationally.

2 Therefore, when all the information is available and time pressure is an issue, the model has little practical use.

3 The routine nature of many jobs means that few decisions actually need to be made and therefore leadership by control rather than discussion is more appropriate.

B | Writing practice

Rewrite thesis statements 1–3 so that the meaning is the same but the words are different.

1 There are a number of different strategies that can be used to make an effective decision.

    _____

    _____

    _____

    _____

2 The traditional office space is unlikely to exist in a few years.

    _____

    _____

    _____

    _____

3 Sharing control is an effective approach a company can use to continue its growth and development.

    _____

    _____

    _____

    _____

Research task

Research another decision-making model and answer the questions.

- Does this decision-making model claim to be the 'best' method for making a decision?
- How does it compare to the decision-making model in this unit?
- Which model, the one you have researched or the one in this unit, do you think is a better model? Why?

12 Innovation

Study focus

1 Rank the innovations in order from 1 (most important) to 5 (least important).

mobile phone ☐   pen ☐

Internet ☐   chair ☐

car ☐

2 Compare your ranking in pairs. Discuss the reasons for the order you chose.

Reading strategies

A | Predicting content using headings

1 You are going to read a text from an academic textbook about marketing. Before you read, match section headings a–e to main ideas 1–5.

  a Creativity and innovation   ——

  b Stimulating innovation   ——

  c Cultures for innovation   ——

  d HR policies for innovation   ——

  e Structures for innovation   ——

  1 Creative people and groups can only generate ideas in the right environment.

  2 Innovative companies have a personnel strategy that promotes training, provides job security and encourages the implementation of new ideas.

  3 The ability to combine ideas in new ways can be used to develop new products and services.

  4 Companies need to be tolerant so people feel they can be creative.

  5 Informal company organizations help to generate new ideas.

2 Compare your answers in pairs then read the text and check your predictions.

B | Reading closely for detailed information

Read the text again and answer the questions.

  1 Who leads the drive for innovation, companies or consumers?

  2 What else is needed, other than just a new idea, for a product to be successful?

  3 According to Figure 1, what is the relationship between input, feedback and output?

  4 According to Figure 2, what three main elements of an organizational context stimulate innovation?

  5 How many features is an innovative culture likely to have?

  6 Which feature of an innovative culture do the following statements describe?

    a Ideas do not have to be realistic or possible.

    b People should not be worried about failure.

    c The target not the method is important.

    d People's efforts need to be noticed.

  7 What is the role of an 'idea champion'?

  8 Name three personality characteristics that an 'idea champion' usually has.

  9 How are the following important for innovation?

    a communication

    b resources

C | Reacting to the text

1 Look at the features of an innovative culture again (lines 32–54). Which features would be the hardest to create for these two companies?

  a a small advertising firm

  b a large corporate bank

2 Would you prefer a job that requires you to be creative or one that lacks creativity? Discuss your reasons in pairs.

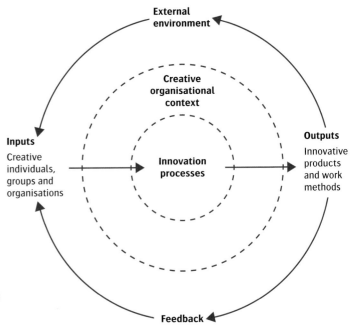

Figure 1: Systems view of innovation

Managing innovation

An increasingly common aspect of managers' jobs is the pressure to stimulate innovation in the areas for which they are responsible. This includes being innovative in creating new products and services, and

5 in the processes that deliver them. Some organisations have developed a reputation for being better than others at sensing and satisfying consumer trends.

Creativity and innovation

Creativity refers to the ability to combine ideas in a new way, or to make unusual associations between

10 ideas. This helps people and organisations to generate imaginative ideas or ways of working: but that in itself does not ensure added value. That only comes when people turn the creative process into products or services that meet a demand, which they can meet

15 profitably. In the public sector innovation is reflected in new ways of delivering services, such as the growing provision of online services.

Stimulating innovation

Figure 1 shows that getting the desired outputs (more innovative products or works methods) depends on

20 both the inputs and the transformation of those inputs. Inputs include having creative people and groups who can generate novel ideas and methods, but creative people can only sustain their creativity in a favourable context. Figure 2 shows three significant elements of

25 that context – cultures, HR policies and structures.

Cultures for innovation

Innovative organisations usually have cultures that encourage experimentation, reward success and accept that some failures are inevitable – a source of learning rather than shame. Robbins and Coulter (2005, p.329)

30 suggest that an innovative culture is likely to have these features:

- *Acceptance of ambiguity* Too much emphasis on objective analysis and detailed planning constrains creativity.
- *Tolerance of the impractical* Individuals who offer

35 impractical, even foolish, answers to speculative questions are not ridiculed. What at first seems impractical may lead to innovative solutions.
- *Low external controls* Rules, regulations and procedures are kept to a minimum.

40 - *Tolerance of risk* Employees are encouraged to experiment without fear of the consequence if they fail. Mistakes become opportunities for learning.
- *Tolerance of conflict* Diversity of opinions is encouraged. Harmony and agreement between

45 people and sub-units is not seen as a sign of high performance.
- *Focus on end rather than means* Goals are clear, but individuals choose how to achieve them.

- *Open systems focus* People are encouraged to monitor

50 the business environment and to be ready to respond to change as it occurs.
- *Positive feedback* Managers provide positive feedback, encouragement and support so employees feel their creativity will receive attention.

HR policies for innovation

55 Innovative organisations actively promote the training and development of their members so that their knowledge remains current. They offer job security to overcome the fear of making mistakes, and encourage people to become 'champions of change'.

60 Such *idea champions* actively and enthusiastically support new ideas. They also build support, overcome resistance, and ensure that ideas are implemented. Idea champions tend to have similar personalities – high self-confidence, persistence, energy and a tendency to

65 take risks. They also inspire and energise others with their vision of the potential of an innovation, through their strong personal commitment to its success. They also need to be good at gaining the support of others – especially those at more senior levels of the

70 organisation.

Structures for innovation

Research into innovation has identified structural factors that encourage it, such as having an organic structure, encouraging horizontal communication, encouraging people to contribute ideas outside their

75 roles, having abundant resources, and frequent communication between units. Organic structures help because they have little formality, work in a

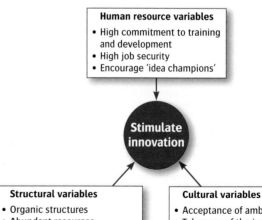

Figure 2: Innovation variables

decentralised way and encourage people to apply skills
and knowledge to a wide range of tasks. This creates
80 an atmosphere of cross-fertilisation and adaptability
that in turn fosters innovation. Abundant resources
help since they enable managers to purchase required
expertise that may have developed in other companies.
It also enables them to take risks by investing in
85 new projects without too much anxiety that failure
will damage the business. Frequent communication
between units fosters the exchange of ideas and
information, which can in turn stimulate combinations
of knowledge, or its application, in unusual ways.
90 Finally, there is evidence that when an organisation's
structure provides explicit support for creativity from
work and non-work activities, an employee's creativity

is enhanced. Support includes encouragement,
open communication, readiness to listen and useful
95 feedback.

Source: P. Baines, C. Fill & K. Page, *Marketing*, Oxford
University Press, Oxford, 2008, pp435–438

Glossary

novel (line 22): new or unusual
horizontal communication (line 73): sharing information
with people at the same level of an organization
abundant (line 75): a lot of
cross-fertilisation (line 80): exchange of ideas and skills
between different people and groups

Business vocabulary

A | Innovation

1 **Complete the table with these verbs.**

stimulate   develop   generate   sustain
encourage   constrain   contribute   foster

to produce or create	*stimulate*
to support and promote	
to maintain	
to control	
to add	

2 **Which words from 1 can collocate with words a–c?**

a ... innovation _____

b ... ideas _____

c ... creativity _____

3 **Choose the best option to complete the sentences.**

a Companies need to have a culture that enables
creative people and groups to _____ imaginative
ideas for new products and services.

1 sustain   2 generate   3 encourage

b Horizontal communication _____ innovation in
the workplace because it allows people to share ideas
and information easily.

1 fosters   2 constrains   3 contributes

c A lack of resources can _____ innovation as
managers might not want to take on the risk of a new
project.

1 develop   2 foster   3 constrain

d It can be difficult to _____ creativity over a long
period of time as people run out of energy.

1 develop   2 encourage   3 sustain

e Job security can help people feel free to _____
new and exciting ideas for innovative products.

1 contribute   2 stimulate   3 foster

4 **Write a sentence for questions a–c using words and
phrases from 1–3.**

a What is the best way to help people create ideas?

b What limits people's ability to create ideas?

c How can a company provide an environment where
people are willing to contribute to innovation?

B | Being innovative

1 **Match words and phrases a–h from the text to
definitions 1–8.**

a enthusiastically support (line 60/61) ___

b build support (line 61) ___

c overcome resistance (line 61/62) ___

d high self-confidence (line 63/64) ___

e persistence (line 64) ___

f inspire (line 65) ___

g energise (line 65) ___

h commitment (line 67) ___

1 to make someone want to do or achieve something
2 to show a lot of positive encouragement
3 when you give time and energy to something you
believe in
4 to make someone feel full of energy or enthusiasm
5 to encourage agreement with an idea
6 to beat opposition towards someone or something
7 a show of determination to not give up
8 a strong personal belief in one's own abilities

2 **Use three of the words or phrases from 1 to describe
you or someone you know.**

Writing skills

Writing a complete essay

This unit revises a number of writing skills from earlier units. You may want to look again at units 5, 6, 9, 10 and 11 to remind yourself of the key ideas.

1 Work in pairs. Read the essay question and brainstorm your ideas on the topic. Use the text to help you.

   A traditional, controlling management structure leads to a lack of innovation. Discuss.

2 Organize your ideas in 1 into a mind map.

3 Order sentences a–e to make an effective introduction to the essay.

   a For continued and sustained success, it is important for companies to continue to innovate. ___

   b Apple was sold for $1 nearly twenty years ago, but went on to become one of the most innovative and successful companies in the world. ___

   c As a result, innovation has become a key element of many managers' roles. ___

   d This essay will first look at the impact of control on innovation and then consider effective ways to stimulate innovation. ___

   e Whilst strict control is important in some aspects of business, it is detrimental to the creative process required for innovation. ___

4 Which sentence in 3 is the thesis statement?

5 Read these two topic sentences from the main body of the essay. Develop them into complete paragraphs, linking the ideas to the thesis statement in 3.

   a There are a number of factors that can lead to a creative environment.

   _____

   _____

   _____

   _____

   _____

   _____

   _____

   b Providing the right managerial structure and work environment is the most effective way to stimulate new ideas.

   _____

   _____

   _____

   _____

   _____

   _____

   _____

6 Work in pairs. Check your partner's paragraphs. Do they contain supporting details and a concluding sentence?

7 Write a conclusion to the essay you have developed in this lesson. Include:

   • a summary of the main ideas
   • a restatement of the thesis

   _____

   _____

   _____

   _____

   _____

   _____

   _____

   _____

8 Check your partner's conclusion.

   • Underline the summary of the main ideas in the essay.
   • Circle the restatement of the thesis.

Research task

Write an essay on the following topic.

Describe the success of an innovative company and analyse the reasons for its success.

Study focus

1 Which of these statements match opinions that are similar to yours and which are different?

Credit card debt is normal.

Buying a house is very important.

If I want something I would rather get a loan now than save for it in the future.

I trust banks to make sensible financial decisions.

2 Do you think your attitude is typical of people from your country or quite different?

3 Do you think attitudes towards the issue of debt are the same everywhere in the world?

Reading strategies

A | Understanding a text using vocabulary and background knowledge

1 The text you are going to read is from the business section of a newspaper. It contains a number of economic terms and concepts. Match a–f to definitions 1–6 then check your answers on page 76.

a deflation _____
b monetary stimulus / quantitative easing _____
c fiscal stimulus _____
d overheating _____
e bond market _____
f bubble _____

1 a temporary situation caused by an increase in prices much higher than the real value of a product
2 policies linked to the supply of money in the economy and the interest rate in the short term
3 policies linked to government spending and taxation
4 the buying of investments (in a government or company) with a promised interest rate – the higher the interest, the greater the risk of the investment
5 for something to grow too much or more than expected
6 a constant long-term fall in prices

2 What do you know about the financial crisis of 2008? Try to answer the questions.

a Why did it happen?
b What problems did it cause?
c Which countries did it start in?
d Did it affect much of the rest of the world?
e Have countries recovered from the situation yet?

3 Read the text and check your ideas in 2.

B | Identifying the writer's point of view

Circle T (true) or F (false).

According to the writer …

1 the worldwide effort during the 2008 crisis prevented disaster. T / F
2 government and central bank response solved the problem completely. T / F
3 the action taken stopped the world entering a period of time similar to the Great Depression. T / F
4 China's response helped the world but not its own economy. T / F
5 China slowing only briefly will not be a problem. T / F
6 it does not matter if China stops its stimulus packages. T / F
7 the US Federal Reserve is very positive about the future. T / F
8 not everyone wants the US government to supply more money. T / F

C | Reacting to the text

1 Now you have read the text, who do you think is to blame for the financial crisis?

a banks   c governments
b individuals   d someone else

2 In pairs, discuss why the group you chose in 1 is to blame.

3 What do you think is the most effective way for a country to move out of recession?

America's century is over, but it will fight on

A "This sucker's going down." That was George Bush's description of the US economy when the financial crisis of 2008 threatened to collapse every bank on Wall Street. International co-operation of a sort never seen
5 before avoided disaster that winter and by the middle of last year the world's biggest economy seemed to be on the mend. American factories started to work again, shares climbed sharply and growth started again. The US was showing its traditional strength when faced
10 with difficulty.

B Central banks and finance ministries concluded that there would be a repeat of the deflationary slump of the 1930s unless they increased the money supply. So they cut interest rates, printed more money and
15 announced large fiscal stimulus packages. This process has worked, but only up to a point. Excluding China, the annual growth rate in the global money supply has fallen from 10% at the height of the financial crisis to zero. Without the action taken
20 by the Federal Reserve, the Bank of England, the European Central Bank and other central banks there would have been a collapse of credit every bit as disastrous as that seen in the Great Depression.

C China's strong capital controls meant most of the
25 benefit from its monetary and fiscal stimulus was felt domestically. Output had recovered quickly and strongly since the collapse in late 2008. As a result this convinced investors that Asia could provide the engine for global growth while North America and Europe
30 gradually recovered. But welcome as it was, China's emergency action was not cost-free. The economy lacked the capacity to cope with the size of the stimulus and showed signs of overheating. Policy has been tightened and China is now showing signs of slowing.

D Provided China slows only briefly there is still a chance that the global economy will recover. Factories in Germany and Japan will produce manufactured goods for Asia. Stock markets will become positive that a second phase of downturn has been avoided. Also
40 cheap money will start to stimulate demand growth in the US once consumers have built up their savings to a level they consider satisfactory.

E But in the US, the Fed is starting to think about a much worse scenario in which the US and Chinese economies
45 stall simultaneously. This will have effects on those countries (a vast number) seeking to export their way out of trouble. The fear, already reflected in global bonds markets, is of softer output, fresh trouble for the banks, and deflation. James Bullard, the president of
50 the St Louis Federal Reserve Bank, noted last week that the US was closer to the deflation seen in Japan in the 1990s than it has been at any other time in its history.

F This is a clear sign that the Fed is considering more quantitative easing this autumn. It probably wouldn't
55 take much more poor economic news to trigger it. It would be a controversial move. Some would argue that the excesses of the bubble years have to be removed from the system. They believe that avoiding the necessary adjustment only prolongs the situation
60 and threatens a burst of inflation. Others believe that the problems of the US economy are too deep seated and irreversible to be solved by regular doses of cheap money.

Source: Larry Elliott, 'America's century is over, but it will fight on', *The Guardian*, 2010

Business vocabulary

A | Economics and finance

Many of the terms in the text on page 53 are common economics and finance terms that are found not only in specialist publications but also the mass media.

1 Find words in the text on page 53 to complete definitions a–h.

   a An investment in s _ _ _ es gives a person a part ownership of a company. (para. A)

   b An i _ _ _ _ es _ r _ _ _ is the extra money a bank charges when you borrow money, or that you receive when you keep money in an account. (para. B)

   c C _ _ _ _ t is another term for debt. (para. B)

   d A d _ _ _ e _ _ _ _ n is a time when there is a lot of poverty and unemployment because there is very little business activity. (para. B)

   e An i _ _ _ _ t _ _ is a person who puts money into something hoping to make more money. (para. C)

   f A s _ _ _ _ m _ _ _ _ t is a place to trade financial products such as shares. (para. D)

   g D _ _ _ _ d is the amount of a product or service people are willing and able to buy. (para. D)

   h To e _ _ _ _ t means to sell goods to another country. (para. E)

2 Complete the text with the words from 1.

Investing in company [1]_____ usually gives a higher profit than the [2]_____ offered by something such as a bank account, especially when the shares are held for a long time. However, the price of shares can go up and down so they do carry risk. When share prices are rising, [3]_____ get very excited and keep buying more shares. The high [4]_____ for the shares can then push the share price higher than its real value. Panic can quickly occur if there are large sales of shares on the [5]_____ . This can lead to a market collapse and a period of [6]_____ and high unemployment. The problem is often made worse by large investors 'leveraging' their investment. In other words, they use [7]_____ to fund their investments. If this is followed by a crash in share prices, together with other economic factors, then a recession can quickly follow. Once a country is in recession, growth is slow unless it can successfully [8]_____ to other countries as a way out of the problem.

B | Economic crisis

1 Complete the table with these verbs.

cope with   trigger   recover   avert
prevent   recoup   handle

before a crisis	
during a crisis	
after a crisis	

2 Match the verbs in 1 to statements a–g. Use the words in *italics* to help.

   a The economy was unable to *deal successfully with* the amount of stimulus and it began to overheat. _____

   b The banks were blamed for *starting* the last recession. _____

   c It will take a long time for many countries' economies to *get better* after the depression. _____

   d Governments have tried to *avoid* disaster by printing more money. _____

   e Many companies had to buy banks to *stop them from* collapsing. _____

   f The company found it difficult to *get back* the money lost as a result of the reduction in trade during the recession. _____

   g The media sometimes makes it difficult for a government to *manage* a crisis. _____

3 Use words and phrases from sections A and B to describe how companies or governments try to deal with economic crisis. Think about:

   • how they can help markets to recover
   • what they could do to recoup government lending
   • how they can handle a crisis

Writing skills

A | Paraphrasing

Paraphrasing is writing the ideas of another person in your own words. It is useful when you are using someone's work to support your own views. When paraphrasing, you need to change the words and the structure but keep the meaning the same. You can:

- replace key words with synonyms
- change the order the information is presented
- change grammatical form and word order

1 Which of these words and phrases can replace the underlined key words and phrases in the sentence below from the text on page 53?

> the summer   at the end of the year   averted
> recovering   largest   unprecedented

International cooperation [1]of a sort never seen before [2]avoided disaster [3]that winter and by [4]the middle of last year the world's [5]biggest economy seemed to be [6]on the mend.

2 Work in pairs. Underline the key words in this sentence from the text. Then think of synonyms to replace the words.

Output had recovered quickly and strongly since the collapse in late 2008.

_____

_____

_____

3 Underline the two pieces of information in this sentence from the text. Then rewrite the sentence so that the information is in a different order.

Output had recovered quickly and strongly since the collapse in late 2008.

_____

_____

_____

4 Look at this sentence from the text and the paraphrase below. Underline changes in grammatical form and circle changes in word order.

Provided China slows only briefly there is still a chance that the global economy will recover.

Providing the Chinese economy slows only briefly there is still a chance the economy of the globe will recover.

5 Look at the paraphrase of this sentence from 1. What has been changed in the paraphrase?

International cooperation of a sort never seen before avoided disaster that winter and by the middle of last year the world's biggest economy seemed to be on the mend.

The biggest economy in the world appeared to be recovering by the summer after unprecedented international cooperation at the end of the year averted disaster.

B | Writing practice

Use the techniques from section A to paraphrase sentences 1–3.

1 American factories started to work again, shares climbed sharply and growth started again.

_____

_____

_____

_____

2 Policy has been tightened and China is now showing signs of slowing.

_____

_____

_____

_____

3 James Bullard, the president of the St Louis Federal Reserve Bank, noted last week that the US was closer to the deflation seen in Japan in the 1990s than it has been at any other time in its history.

_____

_____

_____

_____

Research task

Research another economic crisis from the past. Express the main points in your own words for discussion in class.

Study focus

1 Tick (✓) how often you do these things on the Internet. What else do you use the Internet for?

	often	sometimes	never
shopping			
chatting			
gaming			
research			

2 Write down the first five companies or sites on the Internet that come into your mind. Compare your list with a partner. Explain any of the companies or sites your partner does not know.

Reading strategies

A | Scanning for specific information

Work in pairs. Quickly read the text about Amazon. com from a business magazine. Find what these dates and numbers refer to. Then tell your partner.

Student A

1 30s _____

2 July 16, 1995 _____

3 November 1995 _____

Student B

1 30 days _____

2 $20,000 _____

3 2,300% _____

B | Reading closely for detailed information

Read the first part of the text again (lines 1–44) and answer the questions.

1 Why does Amazon.com stand out above all the other dot-coms?

2 Who originally were the main users of the Internet?

3 How did Bezos finance his business?

4 How long did he test the site for?

5 How did he market the website?

6 What potential did Bezos see in the Internet?

C | Discussing the text

1 The second part of the text (lines 45–84) focuses on six characteristics for successful business leadership. Work in pairs. Student A, read characteristics 1–3. Student B, read characteristics 4–6.

2 Briefly summarize each characteristic in your own words.

3 Rank each of your three characteristics in order from 1 (you think is most important) to 3 (you think is least important).

4 Explain your three characteristics to your partner and the reasons for your order of importance.

5 Together, agree an overall order of importance for all six characteristics.

D | Reacting to the text

Discuss the questions in pairs.

• Why do you think so many new businesses are online businesses?

• Ninety per cent of new online businesses fail. Why do you think this is?

• If you could have an online business, what would it be and why?

• How do you think you could ensure your new business succeeded?

What We Can All Learn From Amazon

Many of the early dot-coms spotted the great opportunities the Internet offered but one company stands out above them all: Amazon.com.

This company anticipated crisis and managed change.
5 It saw beyond the obvious channels of business to what the World Wide Web might mean for global commerce. Its vision was so good it went on to become the world's number one Internet retailer.

Amazon.com's founder, Jeff Bezos, was a graduate with
10 degrees in computer science and electrical engineering. In his 30s, he started to focus on the Internet. There he spotted an opportunity during a time when the Internet was mainly used by academics and government agencies. Seeing beyond the obvious to potential
15 commercial uses, Bezos saw an opportunity in the general public's growing usage of the Internet.

Books, Bezos soon discovered, were ideal. And Amazon's early operation was a typical example of an Internet start-up. Bezos setup shop in a two-bedroom
20 house in Bellevue, Washington. Using limited capital raised from family and friends, he designed, built, and tested the beta-version website. On July 16, 1995, after a successful month of testing, and almost a year after Jeff and Mackenzie arrived in Washington, Amazon.
25 com was launched.

The only marketing was word of mouth, and that was all it took. In 30 days, Amazon.com had sold books into all fifty states and forty-five countries beyond. By November 1995, Amazon.com realized its first
30 100-order day and was doing more than $20,000 in sales each month.

But it was not only this early success that gave Bezos his good fortune. He foresaw the coming wave like almost no one else. He saw that the Internet would
35 grow quickly, that its 1994 growth of 2,300 percent was just the beginning. He saw the potential to transform the Internet into something that would change the way that people did business forever. Today, Amazon.com is still the world's largest Internet retailer, handling not
40 only its own stock and sales but also other numerous major brands. Amazon.com is the story of one man who set his sights on one great opportunity. This vision changed traditional industries, and created one of the most recognizable brands in the world.

45 Amazon is a forward-thinking company. Its relevancy to consumers and businesses will remain strong due to Jeff Bezos' vision and the workplace culture that embodies the six characteristics of the Immigrant Perspective on Business Leadership. These
50 characteristics come from the idea that immigrants experience many new experiences and challenges and are often at a new exciting stage in their life. The six characteristics are:

1 Keep Your Immigrant Perspective: Amazon keeps its
55 cultural perspective by seeking to find new ways to continuously reinvent itself. Today, Amazon is known just as much for its Kindle e-reader devices as it is known for its online store.

2 Employ Your Circular Vision: As noted, Bezos anticipated
60 crisis and managed change in the book industry. He saw the potential for online commerce before almost anyone. He created the online book retailing industry and he continues to see opportunities others don't.

3 Unleash Your Passion: Bezos' leap of faith from Wall
65 Street to his garage in Bellevue, Washington allowed him to create possibilities that he aimed to share with others.

4 Live With An Entrepreneurial Spirit: Since his early days at Fitel, Bezos' entrepreneurial spirit has always
70 remained alive. As such, Amazon's innovations remain endless.

5 Work with a Generous Purpose: Amazon's story is one that involves sharing the harvest of one's success with others. Not only did Amazon share their
75 ecommerce platform with others retailers, they allowed independent authors the means to promote, market and sell their books.

6 Embrace Your Cultural Promise: The Amazon culture strongly accepts the idea that making mistakes is
80 an essential part of pursuing new ideas. At Amazon, everyone is encouraged to have a fearless attitude toward experimentation and the future. This attitude is crucial to Amazon's ongoing success; without it, innovation would wither and die.

85 Amazon stands out among Internet companies in many ways, but the most important is that it has thrived by fully living the entrepreneurial attitude with which it started.

Source: Glenn Llopis, 'What We Can All Learn From Amazon about Seeing Business Opportunities Others Don't See', *Forbes Business*, 2011

Glossary

setup shop (line 19): start a business

leap of faith (line 64): when you do something even though you are not sure it is right or will succeed

harvest of one's success (line 73/74): the successful result of an effort or action

Business vocabulary

A | Starting a new business

1 Match the words in *italics* in the sentences to the correct definition.

   a Jeff Bezos, the *founder* of Amazon, *established* the company in 1995.

     1 the process of starting a company _____

     2 the person who starts a company _____

   b Amazon was a typical *start-up* when it *launched* its website in 1995.

     1 a new small business _____

     2 to introduce something new to the public _____

   c Amazon has *set up* many successful *spin-off* companies with products such as the Kindle.

     1 to start or create _____

     2 a product or service that is based on another one that already exists _____

   d Amazon was such a successful *venture* that it was *floated* on the New York Stock Exchange two years after its launch.

     1 to sell shares in a company to the public for the first time _____

     2 a new business which involves risk _____

2 Complete the sentences with words from 1. Sometimes more than one word is possible.

   a Microsoft was _____ on 4 April 1975 and it was _____ on the stock market in 1986.

   b The Microsoft _____ , like any new business activity, carried risk. However, it was so successful it made some 12,000 millionaires on its first day of trading on the stock market.

   c In 1995, Microsoft _____ its computer operating system Windows 95 and it sold 7 million copies in the first five weeks.

   d Microsoft's _____ , Bill Gates, is famous all over the world today. In addition to Microsoft, he has _____ many _____ companies and products such as the search engine Bing.

   e The company has progressed from a small Internet _____ to one of the most famous brands in the world.

3 Think of a famous company you know well, or research one. Use the words and phrases from 1 to write a brief history of the company.

B | Opportunities

Starting a new business or launching a new product is often related to spotting an opportunity.

1 Match words a–h to definitions 1–8.

   a anticipate (v.)   ___

   b vision (n.)   ___

   c potential (n.)   ___

   d foresee (v.)   ___

   e reinvent (v.)   ___

   f break (n.)   ___

   g envisage (v.)   ___

   h pursue (v.)   ___

   1 a mental image of how something could develop in the future

   2 to change into something different

   3 to imagine and prepare for something happening

   4 an opportunity that helps you be successful

   5 to know about something before it happens

   6 to picture something happening

   7 to try hard to do or achieve something

   8 the possibility to develop or succeed in the future

2 Complete the sentences with words from 1. Sometimes more than one word is possible.

   a The organizers _____ many visitors attending the event, so they are going to hire extra staff.

   b Bill Gates' _____ 'to have a computer on every desk' resulted in the world's biggest software company.

   c Many people have good ideas but not everyone has the motivation to _____ them.

   d He was very adaptable and could _____ himself for any new role or situation.

   e Bezos saw the _____ of the Internet for retail long before many other people.

   f Many of the most successful investors can _____ problems ahead in the market and sell stocks and shares before their value drops.

   g His big _____ came when he was offered a job in a leading investment bank.

   h We don't _____ any difficulties as long as we keep within budget.

3 Write a brief description of someone you feel had a 'vision' or saw a business opportunity. Use words and phrases from sections A and B to describe their success.

Writing skills

A | Referencing

Using the ideas of others strengthens your arguments and demonstrates your knowledge in a field. There are a number of methods for referencing the sources of ideas. This lesson focuses on the Harvard method.

1 Look at quotes a and b, based on this original sentence from a source.

It is the task of management to create the conditions in which individuals may satisfy their motivational needs.

   a According to Mullins (2007: 445), 'It is the task of management to create the conditions in which individuals may satisfy their motivational needs.'

   b According to Mullins (2007), managers need to produce circumstances in which employees can fulfil their motivational needs.

2 What differences are there between the two quotes?

3 What information about the source is included in each quote?

4 Read the definition of an indirect quote. Which quote in 1 is indirect?

An indirect quote uses the ideas of the author but is expressed in your own original words.

5 Complete the definition of a direct quote with these words.

   page number   year   the exact   quotation marks

   A direct quote uses [1]_____ words of the author. We place [2]_____ around the quote to indicate which words were said by the author. We also include the [3]_____ of publication and the [4]_____ where the quote can be found.

6 Indirect quotes tend to be used more than direct quotes. Which two of these reasons are correct?

   a Only very original expressions tend to be kept as a direct quote.

   b Often the English can be improved from the original.

   c Changing it into your own words will help fit the flow of your writing better.

   d The original may have good ideas but poor language.

B | Using reporting verbs

Reporting verbs can be used in academic writing when referring to other people's work. The choice of reporting verb will depend on the point you want to make about what you have read.

1 Underline the reporting verbs in these sentences.

   a Smith (2004) demonstrates that poor marketing results in the failure of many e-businesses.

   b Holly (2008) argues that poor marketing results in the failure of many e-businesses.

   c Nukui (2010) describes five factors that result in the failure of e-businesses.

2 Match the reporting verbs in 1 to meanings a–c.

   a to state strongly that something is true or is a fact _____

   b to say what someone or something is like _____

   c to show that something is true _____

3 Which of these verbs could replace each verb in 1?

   a define _____

   b show _____

   c contend _____

C | Writing practice

The reading text in this unit comes from a website. One difference when referencing a website in writing is that there is no page number. Everything else remains the same. The source information for the text is:

Forbes Magazine, 2011, Glenn Llopis

1 Use the text on page 57 to write a direct quotation to support this statement. Remember to give the source details.

Early dot.com industries could achieve major success.

2 Use the text on page 57 to write an indirect quotation to support this statement. Remember to give the source details.

Entrepreneurship pushes companies forward.

Research task

Find another successful e-business and write a brief explanation about its success. Use vocabulary from this unit and include a direct and indirect quotation from the same source.

Study focus

1 Have you ever been managed by someone? What was positive and what was negative about their management style?

2 Would you like to be a manager? If so, what skills do you have that would make you a good manager? Make a list and compare it with a partner.

3 If somebody says they use a 'carrot and stick' method of management, what do you think they mean?

Reading strategies

A | Reading quickly for general understanding

1 Read the text from an academic textbook about management. Which definition, a or b, matches Theory X and which matches Theory Y?

   a a method of management that allows the worker more control

   b a method of management that emphasizes control

2 Which theory do these ideas relate to? Circle *X* or *Y*.

a	People are lazy.	X / Y
b	People can self-direct.	X / Y
c	People need to be directed and threatened.	X / Y
d	Achievement needs to be rewarded.	X / Y
e	People seek responsibility in the right conditions.	X / Y
f	People lack ambition.	X / Y
g	People lack motivation beyond the very basic level.	X / Y
h	People are creative.	X / Y
i	People's intellect is not fully used.	X / Y
j	Motivation occurs at a high level.	X / Y

B | Identifying arguments for and against

Read the text again. Which argument from each pair does the writer present in the text?

1 Theory X

   a McGregor believes this approach best matches human nature.

   b McGregor does not believe this approach matches human nature.

2 Theory X

   a Using Theory X will have positive outcomes.

   b Using Theory X will have negative outcomes.

3 Theory Y

   a Theory Y will get employees to work with a manager.

   b Theory Y will get employees to work against a manager.

4 Theory X and Y

   a Theory X is the best management method.

   b Theory Y is the best management method.

C | Reacting to the text

Discuss the questions in pairs.

- Which method do you think is the best management method and why?
- The writer is clearly against Theory X. Are there any situations where you think Theory X might have positive outcomes?
- Have you worked for managers with different styles of leadership? If so, do their styles match one of the theories or are they somewhere between the two theories?

Theory X and Theory Y

(a) How managers approach the performance of their jobs and their behaviour towards subordinate staff is likely to be influenced by their ideas about people, and human nature and work. Using Maslow's hierarchy
5 of needs model, McGregor, in 1960, put forward two theories about human nature and behaviour at work. He argued that the style of management adopted is a function of the manager's attitudes towards people and assumptions about human nature and behaviour. The
10 two ideas are called Theory X and Theory Y and are based on polar assumptions about people and work.

Theory X

Theory X represents the carrot-and-stick assumptions on which traditional organisations are based. Its assumptions are that:

15 • (b) the average person is lazy and has a natural dislike of work;

• most people must be coerced, controlled, directed and threatened with punishment if the organisation is to achieve its objectives;

20 • the average person avoids responsibility, prefers to be directed, lacks ambition and values security most of all; and

• motivation occurs only at the physiological and security levels.

25 The central principle of Theory X is direction and control through a centralised system of organisation and the exercise of authority. McGregor questioned whether the Theory X approach to human nature is correct. He also questioned the relevance of
30 management practices which are based upon it.
(c) Assumptions based on a Theory X approach, and the use of rewards and sanctions, could result in an exploitative or authoritarian style of management.

Theory Y

At the other extreme to Theory X is Theory Y which
35 represents the assumptions consistent with current research knowledge. The central principle of Theory Y is the integration of individual and organisational goals. Its assumptions are:

• for most people work is as natural as play or rest;

40 • people will exercise self-direction and self-control for the benefit of objectives to which they are committed;

• commitment to objectives is a function of rewards associated with their achievement;

• (d) given the right conditions, the average worker can
45 learn to accept and seek responsibility;

• the capacity for creativity in solving organisational problems is distributed widely in the population;

• the intellectual potential of the average person is only partially utilised; and

50 • motivation occurs at the belongingness, esteem and self-actualisation levels as well as at the physiological and security levels.

(e) McGregor implies that a Theory Y approach is the best way to elicit co-operation from members of an
55 organisation. It is the task of management to create the conditions in which individuals may satisfy their motivational needs and in which they achieve their own goals through meeting the goals of the organisation.

Managerial strategies

Although Theory X and Theory Y are based on polar
60 extremes and are an over-simplification, they do represent identifiable philosophies that influence managerial behaviour and strategies. Most people have the potential to be self-motivating. They can best achieve their personal goals through self-direction
65 of their efforts towards meeting the goals of the organisation. Broadening educational standards and changing social values mean that people today have wider expectations of the quality of working life, including opportunities for consultation and
70 participation in decisions that affect them. Managers should develop practices based on an accurate understanding of human behaviour and motivation.

....

Source: L. Mullins, *Management and Organisational Behaviour*, Eighth edition, Pearson Education, 2007, pp444–445

Business vocabulary

A | Other people's ideas

In academic writing several different verbs can be used to introduce the ideas of other people.

1 Look at the words in *italics* in sentences 1–8 and answer questions a–c. Use a dictionary to help if necessary.

   a Which three words are used to describe a possibility?

      _____

   b Which three words mean to disagree with strongly?

      _____

   c Which two words mean to express some doubt?

      _____

   1 Smith *intimates* that whilst these conditions are ideal they are not realistic.

   2 McGregor *rejects* the idea that Theory X matches well to natural human behaviour.

   3 His research methods have been *questioned* by many.

   4 McGregor *suggests* that empowering employees is key to creating an effective work environment.

   5 Many have *disputed* the validity of Maslow's theory.

   6 Whilst the ideas were not challenged openly, it was *implied* that there were significant weaknesses.

   7 Even a weak idea can encourage thought and make people attempt to *challenge* it, thus advancing the field.

   8 It is difficult not to *query* the ideas when they are based on little research.

2 Use the information in the text on page 61 and reporting verbs from 1 to write sentences about ideas a–e. Refer to Mullins or McGregor as appropriate. (The information you will need is indicated by a letter in the text.)

   a The way people manage is affected by how they view people.

      Mullins suggests that a manager's behaviour towards staff will be based on their views of people.

   b People are lazy and need to be controlled.

   c Theory X may result in a poor management style.

   d People like to be controlled.

   e The importance of cooperation.

3 Could you replace any of the verbs in the sentences in 2 without changing the meaning?

B | Management styles

1 Match the words in *italics* to definitions a–h.

Attitudes towards management have changed dramatically in recent years. Previous management styles relied heavily on the manager's position to either *threaten* or *coerce* workers into performing. This *assumption* that people performed when pressured or pushed into completing a task appears outdated today. Managers are more likely to *consult* with an employee than to threaten them. Companies try to *utilize* their workforce better by considering employees' interests and strengths when delegating work tasks. These changes mean that power is *distributed* more evenly among members of staff and that companies are *rewarded* with more productive and motivated employees.

   a to say you will cause problems for someone if you do not get what you want

   b to discuss something with someone before making a decision

   c to persuade someone forcefully to do something they do not want to do

   d to use something in an effective way

   e to share something between a number of people

   f feelings or opinions about someone or something

   g to give someone something in return for good work

   h a belief that something is true even though you have no proof

2 Complete the text with the words from 1. Change the form of the word if necessary.

I left my last job because the managers were very authoritarian. They used to [1]_____ us into doing extra work at weekends. They also [2]_____ us with dismissal if they felt we weren't performing at work. Personally, I do not respond well to people with such a negative [3]_____ . I'm much more productive if I'm given responsibility and I'm [4]_____ about any decisions that affect me. The [5]_____ that people need to be bullied into working is very outdated. My new company is much better. They [6]_____ work evenly among the members of the team and they [7]_____ the skills and strengths of each individual. They always [8]_____ work of a high standard, so motivation is high within the team.

3 Briefly describe your opinion of effective management, using words from 1.

Writing skills

A | Using sources in writing

Units 8, 13 and 14 focus on skills related to using the ideas of others in academic writing. This lesson will look at how to bring all those skills together and integrate others' work into your own writing.

1 Making notes is an effective method when you want to use a longer section of another's work in your own writing. Look at the notes for the first paragraph of the text on page 61 and compare them with the original text.

> *Manager's approach comes from beliefs about people, human nature and work.*
> *McGregor = 2 ideas about hum. nat. + work*
> *Style of man. = att. to people*
> *2 ideas are Theory X and Y*

2 Underline two examples of each of these techniques in the notes in 1.

   a using abbreviations
   b using content words
   c simplifying complex sentences
   d using symbols

3 Work in pairs. Make notes on the text on page 61, focusing on key content words, abbreviations and simplifying complex sentences.

   Student A Make notes on the assumptions of Theory X.

   Student B Make notes on the assumptions of Theory Y.

4 Give a spoken summary of your theory to your partner.

5 Expand your notes on your theory into a maximum of two sentences.

6 Paraphrasing is an effective method if you want to focus on a smaller section of another's work. You can change word order, sentence structure and grammatical form, and use synonyms for key words. The meaning stays the same.

   Look at the sentence from the text on page 61 and the paraphrase below. Tick (✓) what has changed:

   meaning   vocabulary   spelling
   grammar   word order

   The central principle of Theory X is direction and control through a centralised system of organisation and the exercise of authority.

   The use of control from a central point and explicit authority are key points of Theory X.

7 Paraphrase this sentence from the text in your own words.

   The central principle of Theory Y is the integration of individual and organisational goals.

8 Both your expanded notes from 5 and your paraphrase from 7 would need to be referenced. Tick (✓) the information you would need to include for an indirect reference in the text.

   a publisher
   b year
   c author's first name
   d author's surname
   e title of the book

   Underline this information in the indirect quote.

   Mullins (2007) describes Theory X as the use of explicit authority and control from a central point.

9 Complete the reporting verbs with the missing letters and put them in the correct group below.

   r _ _ _ _ t   s _ _ g _ _ _   q _ e _ t _ _ _
   im _ _ _   c _ _ _ l _ _ _ e   q _ _ _ y

express possibility	
disagree	
express doubt	

B | Writing practice

Write a paragraph on the topic of Theory X.

- Introduce the topic (check unit 10 if you are not sure how).
- Introduce the quote using a reporting verb.
- Comment on the significance of the quote – what does it show or mean in relation to the paragraph topic?

Research task

Find another theory of management such as Taylor's scientific management theory, Weber's theories of bureaucracy or Fayol's principles of management. Create one paragraph highlighting a key idea in the theory, including an indirect reference.

Study focus

1 List five qualities or skills of a good leader. Share your list with a partner.

2 Do you think these qualities and skills vary from country to country?

3 What additional qualities or skills might someone need to work internationally?

Reading strategies

A | Identifying main ideas

1 Quickly read the text from a business magazine about what makes global leaders successful. Which statement a–d completes this summary of the main idea best?

Successful global leaders …

a are internationally educated.

b face many difficulties due to conflicts around the world.

c need to be flexible, innovative, react quickly, be open to diversity and give autonomy to others.

d need to be well-educated, financially-minded and have a western business mentality.

2 Read the text again. Which sentences correctly give the main idea of the paragraph? Circle *Y* (yes) or *N* (no).

A The world Economic Forum is not concerned about diversity.   Y / N

B Good leaders understand the importance of diversity.   Y / N

C All international companies have a wide range of nationalities in their leadership.   Y / N

D Companies need to be able to respond to uncertain environments.   Y / N

E The world is changing quickly but decisions need to be slow and carefully considered.   Y / N

F Leaders need to be flexible and adapt to market needs and changes.   Y / N

G Leaders need to have similar skills to work successfully together.   Y / N

H Centralized headquarters in charge of everything is important.   Y / N

I Responding positively to changes will enable companies to be successful.   Y / N

3 Correct the incorrect sentences in 2.

B | Identifying supporting ideas

Read the text again, if necessary, and answer the questions.

1 How did the forum in Davos show that diversity is considered to be important?

2 Why do leaders need to be open to ideas from different cultures and geographical areas?

3 How many respondents said that their leadership team has leaders from outside their home country?

4 How do successful leaders capitalize on their global workforce?

5 In what ways can companies react quickly?

6 How would improvisation help a company operate in emerging markets?

7 Why do international and not necessarily local leaders need to be appointed?

8 Why do leaders need to respond positively to change?

C | Reacting to the text

1 Look back at your list from *Study focus*. How do your ideas compare with the ideas in the text?

2 What skills do you have that would make you a good leader?

3 Imagine you were a global leader. How would you rate yourself for each of the leadership tactics described in the text?

Accelerate						
Very poor	1	2	3	4	5	Excellent
Improvise						
Very poor	1	2	3	4	5	Excellent
Select						
Very poor	1	2	3	4	5	Excellent
Empower						
Very poor	1	2	3	4	5	Excellent

4 Compare and discuss your answers in pairs.

E&Y CEO on what makes global leaders successful

A The World Economic Forum put talk of diversity into action this year. It required its strategic partners to bring at least one female member in their five person delegation to Davos. Certainly this was a positive step to strengthen our global conversations with new voices that may have
5 been overlooked in the past.

B Those of us in the private sector should consider similar steps to deal with not only gender issues, but geographical and cultural differences as well. The rise of emerging markets has created a business environment where growth and innovation can come from anywhere. This means that
10 strong leaders must be open to ideas from everywhere. But a new study conducted by Ernst & Young shows the majority of companies struggle to put their beliefs into action.

C In Ernst & Young's latest survey on globalization, we found that the majority of respondents believe diversity of teams and experience
15 improves both the financial performance and reputation of their organizations. However, there is a disconnect. Three out of ten respondents say they have no representatives on their management team or board from outside their home country. On a more positive note, diversity tends to increase in line with overseas sales. Among
20 those companies that get more than 10% of their revenues from other countries, the numbers look very different. Just 22% say they have only home-country representatives on their management team.

D Our research found that the leaders of successful organizations capitalize on the richness of their global workforce. They look for and implement
25 ideas from a variety of individuals with different backgrounds, skills and experiences. And they are not afraid to experiment. This strategy has brought good results for Coke, and it is one of the most effective responses to the new reality. It does not attempt to remove uncertainty in the business world but rather to manage it in ways designed to obtain
30 the best possible outcome. This is no easy task: it takes considerable energy and resourcefulness. But leading companies have fine-tuned the art of responding to uncertainty. Based on their experience, here are four tactics to consider:

E *Accelerate.* In a rapidly changing world, responses and decisions must
35 be swift. Leaders need to be able to process information quickly, incorporate multiple viewpoints and create organizational structures that allow for fast action.

F *Improvise.* Be open to different market characteristics – some markets may grow more slowly than others. Leaders need to innovate rapidly and
40 must seek to learn about other markets and other cultures. In emerging markets, strategies developed over months and years may have to be discarded – and new ones created – at short notice.

G *Select.* Find time to sponsor and appoint rising leaders who don't think, look, or act like you do. Adding diversity to your management team has
45 long-proven advantages. It has been a truism for some years that local executives should run local operations. But a global talent management approach is more sophisticated. Good business leaders choose from a range of diverse candidates with international experience and the ability to operate in markets at different stages of maturity.

H *Empower.* Senior leaders must be willing to give their local market heads considerable authority and decision-making autonomy. However, workplace culture and values will
55 hold the organization together. The traditional practice of transferring entire business models from one market to another, and running everything from a centralized
60 headquarters far away, is no longer relevant. In a global marketplace diverse customers, suppliers and stakeholders all have different needs.

I The concern of many leaders is to
65 find shared norms in a world that is interconnected but also conflicted. In a future that will have immense challenges, leaders who create positive responses to this new reality
70 stand the best chance of creating lasting success for their organizations.

Source: James S. Turley, 'E&Y CEO on what makes global leaders successful', *Fortune*, 2011

Glossary

disconnect (n.) (line 16): when two things do not relate

fine-tune the art of (line 31): to perfect the method of doing something

truism (line 45): a statement that does not need to be made because everyone knows it is true

Business vocabulary

A | Markets

1 Match collocations a–h from the text on page 65 to definitions 1–8.

a strategic partner (line 2) ——
b private sector (line 6) ——
c emerging market (line 8) ——
d business environment (line 8) ——
e market characteristics (line 38) ——
f stage of maturity (line 49) ——
g local market (line 51) ——
h global marketplace (line 61) ——

1 a new and often growing market
2 an area of business not controlled by the government
3 a market limited to one area or one country
4 a point in a market's development
5 a company or person that an organization works with to achieve a common objective
6 the situation in which a company operates
7 the typical qualities of a market
8 a market that is spread throughout the world

2 What is each person talking about? Rewrite the sentences using the collocations from 1.

a 'We need someone to work together with to get us into the market.'

We need a strategic partner to get us into the market.

b 'Our company has traditionally operated just in this country.'

_____

c 'It's the new market everyone wants to invest in.'

_____

d 'The government sold the trains to a number of non-government companies.'

_____

e 'This is a difficult economic situation to operate in.'

_____

f 'The typical qualities of this market that are most attractive are market size and annual growth rate.'

_____

g 'We need to stop thinking so narrowly and aim to compete in the world market.'

_____

h 'The market is past its peak and has reached a point where I think we need to consider our exit strategy.'

_____

B | Word formation and synonyms

The use of synonyms and changing the structure of a sentence to use different forms of a word can add variation to your writing.

1 Look at this paragraph from the text on page 65 and <u>underline</u> any words with a similar meaning.

Accelerate. In a rapidly changing world, responses and decisions must be swift. Leaders need to be able to process information quickly, incorporate multiple viewpoints and create organizational structures that allow for fast action.

2 Use the words you <u>underlined</u> in 1 to replace the words in **bold** in this paragraph. You may need to change the form of the word.

Business is changing **quickly** and companies need to adapt **quickly** to keep up with the change. Any company that is unable to adapt **quickly** is likely to be left behind. Companies that manage to progress **quickly** to meet customer needs will be the most successful.

3 Find words in the text on page 65 that mean 'not the same as'.

a d _ _ _ r _ _ _ y (para. A) _____
b d _ _ _ er _ _ _ es (para. B) _____
c v _ _ _ ety (para. D) _____
d d _ _ _ _ r _ _ t (para. G) _____

4 Complete the table with the different forms of the words.

Verb	Noun	Adjective	Adverb
	diversity	*diverse*	
		different	
	variety		

5 Complete the sentences with the correct form of the words in brackets.

a A company that tries to _____ (vary) its management team will be more successful.
b People who think _____ (different) from the norm may be more creative than others.
c _____ (diversify) is often viewed positively as it brings fresh perspectives on an issue.

Writing skills

A | Writing a draft

Writing a draft essay involves a number of steps from analysing the question through to proof reading. Feedback on your draft will develop your essay further.

1 Number the steps in the writing process in order from 1 (first) to 8 (last).

a Plan your essay. ___

b Write a first draft. ___

c Analyse the question. ___

d Develop research questions. ___

e Brainstorm your ideas. ___

f Proofread your writing. ___

g Conduct your research. ___

h Organize your ideas. ___

2 Work in pairs. Read the essay question and follow steps a–d.

Successful international leaders need to be able to adapt quickly. To what extent do you agree with this statement?

a Analyse the question: What exactly is it asking you to do, e.g. evaluate, describe?

b Brainstorm your ideas: Think of as many different points as possible.

c Organize your ideas: How will you connect the points of your brainstorm together in an essay?

d Develop your research questions: What information do you need to find to be able to answer the essay question?

3 Think about the different parts of an essay and complete tasks a–c.

a Put the following into the correct order for the structure of an effective introduction.

- an indication of the essay's structure ___
- a thesis statement giving the main argument or point of view ___
- more specific information on the essay's topic ___
- interesting the reader by using a quotation, a question, an interesting fact, a definition, or general background information ___

b Put the following into the correct order for the structure of a well-structured paragraph.

- a concluding sentence ___
- a short explanation to support the main idea ___
- a topic sentence giving the main idea of the paragraph ___
- identification of the results/implications of the main idea ___

c Cross (✗) the things which a conclusion should *not* include.

- a summary of the main ideas ___
- a restatement of the thesis from the introduction ___
- predictions ___
- logical conclusions to the argument ___
- closing thoughts on the topic ___
- new information ___

B | Using feedback

Read the feedback from a teacher on a first draft of the essay in section A. Improve the draft.

1 'Your introduction has no clear line of argument.'

Nearly 70% of businesses operate locally, but more than 50% of trade happens internationally. Working in such a large international market obviously presents challenges for leaders. This essay will look firstly at what those challenges are and then at how managers can be effective in this environment.

2 'Your paragraph here contains irrelevant information.'

An ability to adapt is key to success. According to Turley (2011), leaders must adapt quickly and learn from new markets, especially in emerging markets. Appointing leaders with an international perspective is also key. By being able to innovate and adapt, a company can meet changing market needs and not only maintain but also grow their market.

Research task

Conduct research for the essay question in section A1.

Write the essay and bring this to class.

Be prepared to provide feedback to a partner on the structure and organization of their essay.

Answer key

Unit 1 Motivation

Reading strategies

B | Reading closely for detailed information
1 a People are motivated by many needs and these needs exist in a hierarchy.
  b self-actualization
  c safety
  d belongingness
  e physiological
  f esteem
  g No, the needs must be satisfied in order.
  h because of the good pay, benefits and job security
  i belongingness and esteem needs
2 a belongingness   c self-actualization
  b esteem   d safety

Business vocabulary

A | General vocabulary
1 a 3   b 1   c 2
2 a 4   b 2   c 6   d 5   e 3   f 1
3 These words all come from the first 2,000 words most commonly used in the English language and so are considered general vocabulary.
4 1 According to   4 concerned with
  2 reflect   5 valued
  3 desires   6 advancement

B | Satisfaction and development
1 a self-image   d responsibility
  b recognition   e potential
  c status   f ability

Writing skills

A | Using relative clauses
2 Sentence A includes a defining relative clause.
  Sentence B includes a non-defining relative clause.
3 Sentence B uses commas. The commas indicate this is extra information that does not define the main noun. This information can be removed without affecting the main meaning of the sentence.
4 a 1 who, whom, whose   3 where
    2 which   4 that
  b that
  c Which and that are most common because academic writing usually refers to things not people.
5 a Motivation, which means the need or reason for doing something, is key to employee satisfaction. ND
  b Employees who worked for the central bank wanted more recognition for their work. D
  c Employees whose safety needs are being met need to then develop good relationships at work to continue to be motivated. D
  d Countries where unemployment is high are usually most concerned about job security. D

B | Writing practice
1 b My father's company, which is in London, is an accountancy firm.
  c Cambridge, where I work, is a fantastic city.
  d I'll send you a brochure that has all the key information.
  e Our director, with whom I discussed the problem, will call you next week.
2 Possible answers
  a Motivation, which is the enthusiasm for doing something, underlies Maslow's theory.
  b Safety needs, which are the feelings of safety and security, are the second need in Maslow's hierarchy.
  c Self-actualization, which is the highest need, is about meeting one's potential.

Unit 2 Managing conflict

Reading strategies

A | Scanning for specific information
1 a three
  b introduction, balancing conflict and cooperation, styles to handle conflict
  c five
  d Figure 1
2 You are more likely to use the text for essay question b.

B | Interpreting graphically presented data
1 a Figure 1 = Balancing conflict and cooperation
    Figure 2 = Styles to handle conflict
  b It has the ideal balance between conflict and cooperation.
  c at either end of the semi-circle
  d competing
  e accommodating
  f see the text (lines 53–57)
2 Suggested answer
  Figure 1 shows the ideal balance between conflict and cooperation and the varying degrees of staff performance dependent on the amount of conflict and cooperation.
3 The text provides additional information about when and how this model would be useful.

C | Reading closely for detailed information
1 a The challenges are making conflicts known and resolving them.
  b People are separated by time, space and cultural differences.
  c Groupthink is where the group starts to think as one.
  d People are unwilling to express opposite opinions which can result in poor decision making. Some conflict is good for generating ideas.
  e When it is too strong or personal, or is not managed appropriately.
  f It can be damaging to the team's morale and productivity and also affect the exchange of ideas and information.
2 a compromising   d collaborating
  b accommodating   e avoiding
  c competing

Business vocabulary

A | Identifying parts of speech
1

Noun	-tion, -sion, -ment, -ence, -ness, -er, -age, -ship -ism, -ity,
Verb	-ate, -ed, -ize, -fy, -ing
Adjective	-al, -ive, -able, -ant, -ed, -ous, -ful
Adverb	-ly

2 a inevitable = adjective   d leader = noun
   b effectively = adverb   e satisfy = verb
   c cohesive = adjective
3 a leader
   b inevitable
   c cohesive
   d effectively
   e satisfy
4 a beneficial   d cooperation
   b requirement   e accommodating
   c committed   f maintain

B | Decisions and conflict
1 a 6   b 1   c 4   d 3   e 2   f 7   g 5
2 a cohesive team   e handle conflict
   b effectively resolve   f exchange of ideas
   c degree of harmony   g decisive action
   d overall solution

Writing skills

A | Using present and past simple tenses
1 Nearly all of the verbs are in the present simple.
2 a 3   b 2   c 1
3 The writer of the text has mostly used the present simple to show that he believes his ideas are generally true.
4 dealt with, merged, existed, was, had, ran, chaired, didn't expect
   The past simple is used.
5 a dealt with, merged
   b existed, was, had, ran, chaired, didn't expect
6 a suffered   d cooperated
   b develop   e value
   c reflects   f failed, was, required

Unit 3 Work-life balance

Reading strategies

A | Reading quickly for general understanding
1 c
2 a A   b C   c B   d D

B | Identifying the writer's point of view
1 a T   b F   c F   d T
2 b

C | Summarizing a text to focus on main ideas
1 a A good summary should focus on the main ideas not details.
   b Summaries written directly from the text are likely to rely heavily on the language used in the text and potentially cause issues with plagiarism.

3 Suggested answers
   B In the past, men mainly worked and women's roles were largely in the home.
   C Schor's claims are not supported by evidence.
   D Men are generally working less and women are now working more in paid roles. This redistribution of work is placing greater pressures on households as a whole.

Business vocabulary

A | The working environment
1 a 8   b 3   c 5   d 6   e 1   f 7   g 2   h 4
2 1 average hours   5 working hours
   2 full-time employment   6 main responsibility
   3 paid work   7 economic progress
   4 increased wealth

B | Time
1 a manage time   c working time
   b time pressure   d shortage of family time
2 b My main responsibility is managing key accounts.
   c Academic study involves managing time to meet a variety of deadlines.
   d The industrial relations are an important part of a company's philosophy.
   e Charities cannot provide paid work and rely on voluntary workers.

Writing skills

A | Connecting ideas
1

Related ideas and examples	in addition, for instance
Sequence	previously, first
Comparison/Contrast	both, whereas
Cause/Effect	results in, due to

2 a contrast   c effect
   b cause

B | Writing practice
1 a whereas   c for instance
   b therefore   d however
2 Suggested answer
   For instance, in 1962, men worked an average of 52 hours per week whereas in 1999, men worked an average of 40 hours per week. In 1950, 10% of women had paid work. However, 75% of women had paid work in 2000. In addition, in 1955, 2% of men were mainly responsible for the domestic household. However, in 2005, 20% of men were mainly responsible for the domestic household. Furthermore, the average household in 1950 worked 52 hours per week whereas the average household in 2005 worked 70 hours per week. Therefore, households today are under more time pressure.

C | Spelling and punctuation
1 a definitely   d prefer
   b disapprove   e their
   c wonderful

2 a … English language …
  b … its roots …
  c After selling the business, he managed to avoid bankruptcy.
  d Jonathan Sayer, the director of the company, resigned from his position.
  e Maria Stuart, dressed in the grey suit, is the director of the company.

Unit 4 Financial crisis

Reading strategies

A | Understanding a text using background knowledge
1 Answers will vary.
2 A types of financial asset, stock markets
  B speculation, stock markets, recession
  C the 'credit crunch' of 2007/08, US sub-prime lending market
  D the 'credit crunch' of 2007/08, US sub-prime lending market
3/4 Answers will vary.

B | Identifying points to support an argument
A 2   B 1   C 2   D 2

C | Finding support for an opinion
1 b is stronger because the opinion is supported by an expert in the field.
2 a The objects of speculation can be financial assets such as shares, bonds, or currencies, or physical assets such as land, property, or works of art.
  b Euphoria develops as people start to believe that the upward movement in prices will always continue.
  c The resulting fall in prices causes panic in the market with investors rushing to off-load their assets leading to a market collapse.
  d House prices were rising and financial institutions were happy to lend to borrowers with poor credit histories.
  e Banks wrote off large amounts of assets and central banks had to put in billions of dollars to prevent the credit system from failing completely.

Business vocabulary

A | Verb + preposition collocation
1 a 2   b 1   c 4   d 5   e 3
2 a put in   d spread across
  b caused by   e characterized by
  c put together

B | Phrasal verbs
1 a 2   b 3   c 4   d 5   e 1
2 a caused by   e put together
  b write off   f based on
  c face up to   g spread across
  d characterized by   h pay back

C | Finance
1 a 1 share   2 bond
  b 1 loan   2 borrower
  c 1 risk   2 losses
  d 1 liquidity 2 bankruptcies
2 The expression means that it is not a good idea to either borrow money from someone or lend it to someone.

Writing skills

A | Writing a descriptive text
1 a 2   b 1   c 3
2 a underlined
  b highlighted
3 a 2   b 4   c 3   d 5   e 6   f 1
4 a spread – present simple
  b The writer believes he is writing about something that is generally true.
5 a A: were taken   B: did not keep
    Sentence A uses the past simple form of be and the past participle of take. Sentence B uses the past simple form of keep.
  b The passive is formed by using the verb be and the past participle.
  c No. Yes.
6 a is caused   b is written off   c is based   d issue

B | Writing practice
Possible answers
1 Speculation is the buying and selling of assets in the hope of making a profit.
2 A financial crisis can be caused when prices increase to a high level and then fall rapidly when people panic.
3 The New York Stock Exchange is in Wall Street in New York City, USA. It is the world's largest stock exchange.

Unit 5

Reading strategies

A | Identifying topic sentences
1 A Every product or service is aimed at a group of target consumers with particular characteristics.
  B Age has a noticeable effect on the needs of consumers in many areas.
  C In the USA, from the 1920s while the Model T Ford had 55% of the car market, General Motors chose a very different strategy to divide its brands according to the age of its customers.
  D Every marketing manager is always looking for the most relevant and operational criteria for building a target market.
2 A 2   B 1   C 1   D 2
3 According to the text, the topic sentence is always the first sentence of the paragraph. Sometimes it can be the second sentence.

B | Identifying main and supporting ideas
A explanation + examples
B explanation + examples
C explanation + examples
D details + explanation

C | Drawing conclusions from a text
1 a D   b A   c B   d C
2 b

Business vocabulary

A | Marketing and segmentation

1 a segmentation d target g campaign
   b enter e trend h image
   c strategy f characteristic i consumer
2 Answers will vary.

B | Noun + *of* + noun

1 a 5 b 1 c 3 d 7 e 2 f 4 g 6
2 1 consumption of products or services
   2 needs of consumers
   3 standard of comfort
   4 approval of society
   5 stage of a person's life
   6 target age of consumer
   7 leader of its market sector

Writing skills

A | Writing comparisons

1 … with biological age. <u>On the other hand</u>, the consumption of cultural services … will be <u>much more</u> influenced by …
2 On the other hand, much more
3 Age has … many areas. <u>On the other hand</u>, other markets stay fairly <u>similar</u> … allows for <u>more</u> precise, and therefore <u>more</u> effective …
4 similar, more
5

Similarities	*neither … nor, as … as, similarly, also, both*
Differences	*in contrast to, whereas, compared with, in comparison with, instead, on the other hand, rather*

6 a as … as d Likewise/Similarly
   b In contrast to e Rather
   c whereas
7 Answers will vary.

B | Writing topic sentences

1 a 2 b 1
2 Possible answers
   a English is the world's global language.
   b Coca-Cola is one of the world's leading brands.

Unit 6

Reading strategies

A | Predicting content using titles and topic sentences

1 b is the most likely because of the words *society* and *culture*.
2 Answers will vary.

B | Reading closely for detailed information

1 beliefs, values, customs, common behaviours, religion, language, non-verbal communication, food, dress
2 He studied over 100,000 workers in IBM companies in 40 countries. He found that the rules and values set in national culture were a very powerful influence on the workplace, and that different approaches would be necessary when managing people from different cultural backgrounds.

3 Western people focus more on detail while Eastern people tend to look at things as a whole.
4 different social environments
5 They can affect things such as agendas and the normal structure of meetings.
6 similarities and differences between cultures

C | Using the text in writing

1 b
2 a Culture is dynamic, in other words it changes over time especially due to the process of globalization with the increasing movement of products, services, and capital between countries, and the migration of people (Dahl).
   b Cultural attitudes can have important implications for business.
   c He argues that countries, especially big countries like China, India, Indonesia, and Brazil do not have a single national culture but many cultures that vary from region to region.
   d Psychologists have shown that Eastern and Western cultures can vary significantly in terms of perception, logic, and how they see the world around them.
   e Similarities between the domestic and foreign cultural rules and values may make entry for a firm easier.

Business vocabulary

A | Understanding the function of vocabulary patterns

1 paragraph A
2 b
3 a culture
   b beliefs, values, customs, and behaviours common in society
   c the increasing movement of products, services, and capital between countries, and the migration of people

B | Culture and the world

1 a exports e regions
   b Globalization f ethnic group
   c multinational g Migration
   d national
2 Answers will vary.
3 attitudes explanations context differences rules
4 a cultural explanations d cultural background
   b cultural rules e cultural context
   c Cultural differences
5 Answers will vary.

Writing skills

| Concluding sentences

1 a 1 b 2, 3, 4 c 5
2 A C B L C L D L E L
3 b The methods used by Americans to conduct business in Japan are influenced by cultural distinctions.
   c The most successful companies pay attention to cultural differences.
4 a argument b argument c description
   Possible concluding sentences
   a Therefore, on this basis English could be considered a global language.
   b Therefore, to be successful in each of these cultures or any culture would require a knowledge and understanding of different expectations.
   c These three factors are the main economic challenges facing Britain today.

Unit 7 Job security

Reading strategies

A | Identifying the main argument
1 c   2 b   3 b   4 a

B | Identifying specific opinions
Suggested answers
1 they can lead to opportunities if workers are able to take advantage of them
2 is common
3 feel unvalued and unneeded
4 negative
5 a loss of valuable time, not applicable to the workplace
6 able to take advantage of new opportunities
7 their own future
8 varied
9 interesting, they have more control

Business vocabulary

| Prefixes
1 a out   b down   c in   d up   e en   f under
  g over   h re
2 a downsizing   b upgrade   c enable   d retraining
  e outsourcing   f insecurity   g overworked   h understaffed
3 a out   b in   c en   d re   e under   f down
  g up   h over
4 a outsourcing   b downsizing   c incomplete   d upgrading
  e enabled   f Underfunded   g overworked   h Retraining

Writing skills

A | Generating ideas
Answers will vary.

B | Organizing ideas
1 a insecurity
  b change, loss of job, retraining
2

Unit 8 Sharing control

Reading strategies

A | Scanning for specific information
1 Possible answers
  Student A
  Randall Bennett: founded Secure Enterprise Computing
  Eric Schmidt: was hired by Google when it expanded
  Phil Dur: managing director of Investor Growth Capital
  Peter Cobb: co-founded eBags
  Student B
  Robert Pickens: was hired as president and chief operating officer of Secure Enterprise Computing
  Sheryl Sandberg: was hired by Mark Zuckerberg of Facebook
  Melinda Emerson: author of *Become your own boss in 12 months*
  Jon Nordmark: previous CEO of eBags

B | Reading closely for detailed information
1 A T   B T   C F   D F   E F   F T   G T
  H F
2 C He could spend more time on developing new business.
  D It's common but difficult.
  E Introducing new management needs to be done carefully.
  H The future is important but the past needs to be appreciated.
3 Possible answer
  Sharing control is difficult but when done carefully it is beneficial for companies and leads to growth.

Business vocabulary

A | Control
1 a 7   b 2   c 4   d 3   e 6   f 5   g 1
2 1 share control   5 give up control
  2 second set of hands   6 authority
  3 leadership team   7 autonomy
  4 head up
3 Answers will vary.

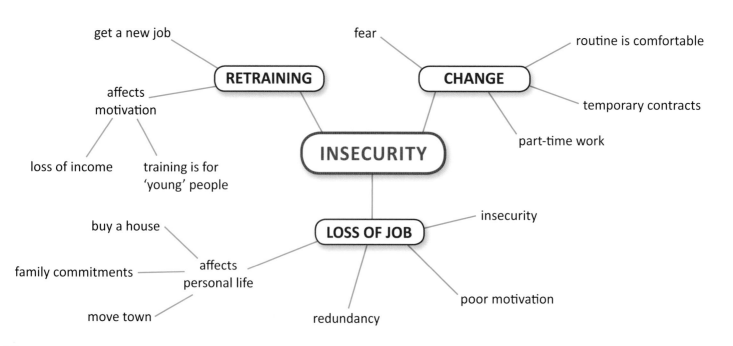

B | Developing a business

1

The start of a business	*build the business, found, co-founder*
The development of a business	*build the business, grow, expand, develop, growth plan*
The time when a business is most successful	*reach a peak*

2
- a co-founders
- b reach a peak
- c grow/expand
- d develop
- e founding
- f growth plan
- g expand/grow
- h built the business

3 Possible answer

H. William co-founded the business in 1995 with J. Maynard. Between 2000 and 2012, sales grew from €1 million to reach a peak of €3 million in 2010 before falling to €2.7 million in 2012. The growth plan for 2013 is to expand the business by increasing staffing by 15% and raising production by 20%. They also aim to grow their retail operations by opening new stores in New York and Hong Kong.

Writing skills

A | Taking notes from a text

2
- a sec. tech. lead. cont.
- b ↑ ↓, =, %
- c Business, Demand, opportunity, expand, team, entrepreneurs, fail
- d 100% nothing or 50% millions, not give up cont. = entrepreneurs fail

3 Possible answers
- b bus.
- c cmp.
- d imp.
- e inv.

4
- a more/greater than
- b pounds
- c does not equal
- d number

5
- a The key content words are mostly nouns and adjectives.
- b All are possible, but sentences 3 and 4 are most likely to be simplified.

B | Expanding notes

2
- a Yes.
- b Yes.
- c Yes, to a certain extent.

3 Possible answers

Business ↑ ↓ – Business had gone up and down.
Demand for sec. tech. = peak means not miss opportunity = expand lead. team – Demand for secure technology was peaking and it was a chance not to be missed so the leadership team was expanded.
100% nothing or 50% millions – You can potentially have 100% of nothing or 50% of millions by expanding your team.
not give up cont. = entrepreneurs fail – Not giving up control can lead to entrepreneurs failing.

4 Answers will vary.

Unit 9 Operations management

Reading strategies

A | Reading quickly for main ideas

1 b
2 a 3   b 1   c 4   d 2

B | Identifying the writer's point of view

1 c   **2** b   **3** c   **4** c

Business vocabulary

| Competition, status and success

1
- a widely recognized
- b win a share
- c set standards
- d achieve
- e widely established
- f compete effectively

2 Answers will vary.

3
- a potential
- b competitive position
- c guarantee of success
- d continuous improvement
- e benefit
- f competitiveness

4
- a guarantee of success
- b potential
- c competitiveness
- d continuous improvement
- e benefit
- f competitive position

Writing skills

A | Writing an effective introduction

1
- a the importance of operations management in the success of a product
- b Possible question: To what extent is operations management important in the success of a product?
- c the relative importance of factors affecting the success of a product
- d to discuss the importance of operations management in relation to other aspects in the success of a product

2
- a Many people put the success of Mercedes down to the design and engineering of its products.
- b Whilst this is a key factor in its success, a number of other factors impact on the company's ability to achieve its aims and objectives. Strategic decisions such as what to produce, where and when are equally key to the quality of what is produced.
- c This essay will argue that without successful operations management a company may fail no matter how good its product is.
- d Firstly, this essay will look at factors affecting success and then evaluate the relative importance of each of these.

3 a 5   b 2   c 1   d 4   e 3

B | Writing practice

1 Possible answers
- a Many departments claim to have the position of greatest importance within a firm and one department that could lay claim to this is that of operations management. Traditionally the role of this department was seen to be of greatest use in the production sector as there are clear measurable targets. However, this essay will argue that operations management can play a key role in any industry including the service industry. This essay will first define operations management and then look at its role in both the production and service sector.

b Some of the fastest growing economies in the world have grown rapidly based on the ability to export. However, such large international trade requires efficient organization and planning of a number of factors. As a result of this globalization, operations management has an even greater role to play in the successful running and management of an international firm. This essay will firstly look at developments in world trade followed by an analysis of the role that operations management can play in this.

Unit 10 Working environment

Reading strategies

A | Understanding a text using background knowledge
Answers will vary.

B | Identifying arguments for and against
A increased productivity and lower costs
B for – mobile staff, work remotely and across time zones, save money, increase flexibility and worker productivity
C They can slow work down.
D choice of how and where to work, balance individual work and interaction, combine face-to face and virtual collaboration
E It gives examples of successful companies who use hybrid work spaces to increase flexibility of office space.
F challenges in the design and construction of workplaces
G Face-to-face interactions and unplanned meetings speed up the decision-making process.

Business vocabulary

A | Pronoun referencing
2 a ... by striking a balance that combines virtual and physical work and space. This could eventually increase ...
  b ... open environments can slow down work. We also know that they can promote ...
  c The mobility we now have allows individuals to choose how and where they work best.
3 a 1 the workplace
     2 the workplace being no longer one fixed location
     3 major developments in the technology used in the workplace
  b 4 these
     5 this
     6 it

B | Change
1 a 2   b 3   c 1   d 4
2 a noun   b verb
3 a rise   e decline
  b increase   f reduce
  c fluctuate   g fall
  d decrease   h drop

4

| small or slow change | minimal, slight, gradual, steady |
| quick or large change | sudden, rapid, sharp, steep, marked, dramatic |

5 b gradual/steady   d gradual/steady
  c minimal   e sharp / marked / dramatic

Writing skills

A | Structuring a paragraph
1 a 4   b 2   c 1   d 3
2 a 2   b 1   c 3   d 4

B | Writing practice
1 Possible answers
  A Companies can gain significant benefits by encouraging innovative uses of space. For example, companies can cut costs, increase flexible working and allow people to work remotely. One example is the use of 'touchdown spaces' where mobile workers can use a workstation only when they need it. Consequently, a firm cannot only cut running costs but also have a more adaptable and flexible workforce.
  B A solely virtual work environment has a number of disadvantages. It has been proven that face-to-face communication is one of the most effective communication methods. In particular it can be useful for making quick decisions and for the creativity that stems from spontaneous meetings. Therefore, all companies should consider providing at least some fixed office space.

Unit 11 Decision making

Reading strategies

A | Identifying main ideas
1 to influence the quality and acceptability of decisions
2 five – autocratic, information seeking, consulting, negotiating, group
3 no
4 seven
5 flexible in the style they adopt
6 It is used in management training sessions to make managers aware of their preferred style and other styles they can adopt to suit different situations.

B | Identifying supporting detail
1 by the manager choosing how best to involve subordinates in decision making and being willing to change their style to match the situation
2 when time is short or the decision is minor
3 so that the style is appropriate to the situation
4 so that managers become more systematic and planned in the decision-making style used

C | Understanding the relationship between text and graphic
1 paragraphs B and D
2 on the decision tree
3 at the top of the figure
4 four
5 four
6 The figure implies that some styles are more frequently useful; the text states the opposite.
7 Possible answer: Decision making can be systematic and a number of key questions can be asked to reach the right decision in the right situation.

Business vocabulary

A | Word formation

1 a 4   b 2   c 3   d 5   e 1

2 and 3

Noun	Adjective	Adverb
acceptance	accepting, accepted, acceptable	
consultation, consultant	consultative	
evaluation	evaluative	
implementation		
preference	preferable	preferably

4 a acceptable   d implementation
   b consultation   e preferably
   c evaluate

B | Leadership and decision making

1 a autocratic   d consult
   b delegate   e criteria
   c negotiate   f subordinates
2 a goals   b democratic   c evaluate   d implement
   e accept
3 Answers will vary.

Writing skills

A | Writing a conclusion

1 sentence 2
2 a 3   b 1   c 4
3 a 2   b 1   c 3

B | Writing practice

Possible answers
1 Effective decisions can be made using a range of decision-making strategies.
2 It is unlikely in the future that people will work in office spaces similar to their current ones.
3 Growth and development can effectively be continued by distributing control between a wider group.

Unit 12 Innovation

Reading strategies

A | Predicting content using headings

1 a 3   b 1   c 4   d 2   e 5

B | Reading closely for detailed information

1 consumers
2 turning the creative idea into something that meets a demand
3 Input creates the product which is the output; customers then feedback in to new or revised inputs and outputs.
4 structural variables, cultural variables, HR variables
5 eight
6 a tolerance of the impractical
   b tolerance of risk
   c focus on end rather than means
   d positive feedback

7 to actively and enthusiastically support new ideas, build support, overcome resistance and ensure that ideas are implemented
8 high self-confidence, persistence, energy and a tendency to take risks (they also inspire and energize others with their vision of the potential of an innovation and are good at gaining the support of others – especially those at more senior levels)
9 a Communication across teams fosters the exchange of ideas and information, which can stimulate innovation.
   b Abundant resources enable managers to purchase expertise and to take risks by investing in new products.

Business vocabulary

A | Innovation

1

to produce or create	develop, generate
to support and promote	encourage, foster
to maintain	sustain
to control	constrain
to add	contribute

2 a stimulate, encourage, constrain, foster
   b develop, generate, encourage, constrain, contribute, foster
   c stimulate, develop, generate, sustain, encourage, constrain, foster
3 a 2   b 1   c 3   d 3   e 1
4 Answers will vary.

B | Being innovative

1 a 2   b 5   c 6   d 8   e 7   f 1   g 4   h 3
2 Answers will vary.

Writing skills

| Writing a complete essay

1/2   Answers will vary.
3 a 2   b 1   c 3   d 4   e 5
4 sentence e
5 Possible answers
   a There are a number of factors that can lead to a creative environment. According to Robbins and Coulter (2005), there are eight factors which can have a positive impact on creativity. Largely these can be summarized as encouraging experimentation, accepting failure and rewarding success. A company that can provide such an environment is likely to be more successful in stimulating innovation.
   b Providing the right managerial structure and work environment is the most effective way to stimulate new ideas. This includes encouraging communication between teams and a less rigid hierarchy (Boddy, 2007). Teams that work in such an environment are likely to be able to build on and develop new and innovative ideas. Without such a system, new ideas are less likely to be successfully brought to market.

7 Possible answer

Allowing teams to experiment, accepting failure and rewarding success are key steps in the innovative process. Creating an environment where communication is open and the hierarchy less rigid is likely to encourage this. Strict control is likely to be detrimental to innovation. Therefore, management that is more willing to relinquish control is more likely to build an innovative environment.

Unit 13 Economics

Reading strategies

A | Understanding a text using vocabulary and background knowledge

1 a 6   b 2   c 3   d 5   e 4   f 1
2 Possible answers
  a banks lending to people with poor credit histories then selling the debt on combined with other debts, so that no one knew who had the bad debt
  b The banking system nearly collapsed and many economies went into recession.
  c US and UK
  d Yes, much of the world.
  e At the time of writing, no.

B | Identifying the writer's point of view

1 T   2 F   3 T   4 F   5 T   6 F   7 F   8 T

Business vocabulary

A | Economics and finance

1 a shares
  b interest rate
  c Credit
  d depression
  e investor
  f stock market
  g Demand
  h export
2 1 shares   5 stock market
  2 interest rate   6 depression
  3 investors   7 credit
  4 demand   8 export

B | Economic crisis

1

before a crisis	trigger, avert, prevent
during a crisis	cope with, handle
after a crisis	recover, recoup

2 a cope with   e prevent
  b trigger   f recoup
  c recover   g handle
  d avert
3 Answers will vary.

Writing skills

A | Paraphrasing

1 1 unprecedented   4 the summer
  2 averted   5 largest
  3 at the end of the year 6 recovering

2 Output had recovered quickly and strongly since the collapse in late 2008.
  Possible synonyms:
  Output = Production
  recovered = got better / improved
  quickly = swiftly / rapidly
  strongly = well
  collapse = fall
  in late = at the end of
3 [1]Output had recovered quickly and strongly [2]since the collapse in late 2008.
  Since the collapse in late 2008 output had recovered quickly and strongly.
4 grammatical form: Provided / Providing; China / Chinese
  word order: global economy / economy of the globe
5 key words, order of information, grammatical form, word order

B | Writing practice

1 Possible answers
  1 Share prices rose rapidly and growth began again when American industry began working again.
  2 The Chinese economy appears to be slowing again since policy became tighter.
  3 James Bullard, the president of the St Louis Federal Reserve Bank, said the previous week that the US economy was nearer to deflation, similar to Japan in the 1990s, than at any other point in its history.

Unit 14 Process of change

Reading strategies

A | Scanning for specific information

1 Student A
  1 the period of his life when Bezos focused on the Internet
  2 Amazon.com was launched
  3 Amazon's first 100-order day and making $20,000 per month in sales
  Student B
  1 sold books into all 50 states and 45 other countries
  2 the amount of sales per month
  3 the growth of the Internet in 1994

B | Reading closely for detailed information

1 It saw what the Internet might mean for global commerce.
2 academics and government agencies
3 by borrowing money from family and friends
4 one month
5 word of mouth
6 something that would change the way business is done forever

Business vocabulary

A | Starting a new business

1 a 1 established   2 founder
  b 1 start-up   2 launched
  c 1 set up   2 spin-off
  d 1 floated   2 venture
2 a established/set up, floated
  b venture
  c launched
  d founder, set up/established, spin-off
  e start-up
3 Answers will vary.

B | Opportunities

1 a 3   b 1   c 8   d 5   e 2   f 4   g 6   h 7
2 a anticipate/foresee
  b vision
  c pursue
  d reinvent
  e potential
  f envisage/foresee/anticipate
  g break
  h foresee/anticipate
3 Answers will vary.

Writing skills

A | Referencing

2 a This includes the page number and quotation marks to show that it is a direct quotation.
  b This changes the wording but keeps the ideas the same. Only the author's surname and year are included because it is an indirect quotation.
3 a author's surname, year, page and quotation marks
  b author's surname and year
4 quote b
5 1 the exact words
  2 quotation marks
  3 year
  4 page number
6 a correct
  b incorrect – It is not a case of making the original better/different but more like the essay writer's own work.
  c correct
  d incorrect – The original is unlikely to be poor English but it is often better to express it differently to fit the flow of your work better.

B | Using reporting verbs

1 a demonstrates   b argues   c describes
2 a argues   b describes   c demonstrates
3 a describe   b demonstrate   c argue

C | Writing practice

1 Possible answer
  Early dot.com industries could achieve major success. Llopis (2011) states that 'Many of the early dot-coms spotted the great opportunities the Internet offered but one company stands out above them all: Amazon.com.'
2 Llopis (2011) demonstrates how entrepreneurship can push a company forward, highlighting the constant innovation of Amazon as an example.

Unit 15 Managing people

Reading strategies

A | Reading quickly for general understanding

1 a Theory Y
  b Theory X
2 a X   b Y   c X   d X   e Y   f X   g X
  h Y   i Y   j Y

B | Identifying arguments for and against

1 b   2 b   3 a   4 b

Business vocabulary

A | Other people's ideas

1 a intimate, suggest, imply
  b reject, dispute, challenge
  c question, query
2 Possible answers
  b McGregor implies that Theory X management views workers as lazy and needing control.
  c McGregor questions the effectiveness of Theory X as a management style.
  d McGregor disputes the idea that people like to be controlled.
  e McGregor intimates that a Theory Y approach is the best way to elicit cooperation from members of an organization.
3 Using a similar word from 1 should allow the verb to be changed without the meaning being changed.

B | Management styles

1 a threaten
  b consult
  c coerce
  d utilize
  e distribute(d)
  f attitudes
  g reward(ed)
  h assumption
2 1 coerce
  2 threatened
  3 attitude
  4 consulted
  5 assumption
  6 distribute
  7 utilize
  8 reward
3 Answers will vary.

Writing skills

A | Using sources in writing

2 a hum., nat., man., att.
  b Manager's, approach, beliefs, human nature, work, Style, ideas, Theory
  c Arguably all of them, but the third one is the most simplified complex sentence.
  d =, +
3 Possible answers
  Theory X
  Av. person = lazy + dislikes work
  Most people must be controlled and threatened to meet objectives
  Av. person = avd responsibility, prf 2 b directed, lck ambition, val. security
  Motivation = physiological + security level
  Theory Y
  self-direction + self-control when committed
  commitment linked to rewards
  Av. worker seeks responsibility
  Creativity distributed widely
  Av. person intellect not fully used
  Motivation at all levels
5 Possible answers
  Theory X
  The average person is lazy, dislikes work and needs to be threatened and controlled to meet objectives. Average people do not want responsibility, prefer direction, lack ambition and are satisfied by meeting basic physiological needs such as security.

Theory Y
People will show self-control and direction when committed to and rewarded for meeting company goals. Workers seek responsibility, are creative and need to be challenged intellectually as they have many motivational needs.

6 vocabulary, grammar, word order
7 The bringing together of personal and company aims are integral aspects of Theory Y.
8 b, d
<u>Mullins (2007)</u> describes Theory X as the use of explicit authority and control from a central point.
9

express possibility	*suggest, imply,*
disagree	*reject, challenge,*
express doubt	*question, query*

B | Writing practice
Possible answer
McGregor's management theory divided management methods into two main groups: Theory X and Theory Y. Mullins (2007) describes Theory X as that of a carrot and stick method whereby employees need to be directed and controlled by a central authority figure. This theory implies that people are not motivated to work and need to be rewarded or punished in order to be motivated. Theory Y could be considered to be the opposite of this.

Unit 16 International success

Reading strategies

A | Identifying main ideas
1 c
2/3 A N – It is concerned about diversity.
B Y
C N – Companies have low levels of diversity unless they have high sales overseas.
D Y
E N – Decisions need to be made quickly.
F Y
G N – People with a diverse range of skills need to be hired.
H N – Local branches should be empowered.
I Y

B | Identifying supporting ideas
1 by requiring at least one in five representatives from each company to be a woman
2 because growth and innovation can come from anywhere
3 seven out of ten, with an increase if sales come from abroad
4 by using a range of people with different backgrounds, skills and experience
5 process information quickly, include a range of views and create structures that allow for fast action
6 by being able to adapt at short notice
7 because they have the ability to operate in a range of markets
8 to stand a chance of being successful

Business vocabulary

A | Markets
1 a 5   b 2   c 1   d 6   e 7   f 4   g 3   h 8
2 b Our company has traditionally operated just in local markets.
c It's the emerging market everyone wants to invest in.
d The government sold the trains to a number of private sector companies.
e This is a difficult business environment to operate in.
f The market characteristics that are most attractive are market size and growth rate.
g We need to stop thinking so narrowly and aim to compete in the global marketplace.
h The market is past its peak and has reached a stage of maturity where I think we need to consider our exit strategy.

B | Word formation and synonyms
1 rapidly, swift, quickly, fast
2 All are possible but try to have a different word for each one. *Swift* will also need to change to *swiftly* in all cases.
3 a diversity   c variety
  b differences   d different
4

verb	noun	adjective	adverb
diversify	*diversity*	*diverse*	*diversely*
differentiate	*difference*	*different*	*differently*
vary	*variety* *variation* *variant*	*various* *varied*	*variously*

5 a vary
  b differently
  c Diversity

Writing skills

A | Writing a draft
1 a 6   b 7   c 1   d 4   e 2   f 8   g 5   h 3
2 a The question is asking you to evaluate the statement and to say how important adaptability is.
3 a 1 interesting the reader …
    2 more specific information …
    3 a thesis statement …
    4 an indication of the essay's structure
  b 1 a topic sentence …
    2 a short explanation …
    3 identification of the results/implications …
    4 a concluding sentence
  c new information ✗

B | Using feedback
Possible answers
1 A thesis statement needs to be added, e.g. Therefore, managers need to be trained in the skills required to operate internationally.
2 The following sentence is off topic: Appointing leaders with an international perspective is also key. Possible revised sentence: Emerging markets can change quickly and companies need to be able to react to this.

OXFORD
UNIVERSITY PRESS

ACKNOWLEDGEMENTS

*The authors and publisher are grateful to those who have given permission to reproduce
the following extracts and adaptations of copyright material:* p.5 and 9 From DAFT.
New Era of Management, International Edition, 9E. © 2010 South-Western, a
part of Cengage Learning, Inc. Reproduced by permission www.cengage.
com/permissions; p.13 *Politics of Working Life* by Edwards & Wajcman (2005)
564 words from pp.44–47. By kind permission of Oxford University Press;
p.17 and 25 *International Business Environment* by Hamilton & Webster (2009)
1397 words from pp.151–152, 154–155, 294–296. By permission of Oxford
University Press; p.21 Extracts from *50+ Marketing* by Jean-Paul Tréguer.
Reproduced by kind permission of Jean-Paul Tréguer; p.29 Extract from
Business Studies by Ian Marcousé. Copyright © 1999, 2003 Ian Marcousé, Andrew
Gillespie, Barry Martin, Malcolm Surridge, Nancy Wall, Marie Brewer, Andrew
Hammond, Ian Swift, Nigel Watson (© 1999 Clive Ruscoe). Reproduced by
permission of Hodder Education; p.33 From 'Expanding management: The
delicate art of sharing control' by Katherine Reynolds Lewis from *Fortune*
magazine, 24 January 2011 © 2011 Time Inc. Used under licence. *Fortune* and
Time Inc. are not affiliated with, and do not endorse products or services of
Oxford University Press; p.37 Extract from *Business Studies* by Ian Marcousé.
Copyright © 1999, 2003 Ian Marcousé, Andrew Gillespie, Barry Martin,
Malcolm Surridge, Nancy Wall, Marie Brewer, Andrew Hammond, Ian Swift,
Nigel Watson (© 1999 Clive Ruscoe). Reproduced by permission of Hodder
Education; p.41 From 'What will the future workplace look like? By Andrew
Laing from Fortune magazine, 19 January 2011 © 2011 Time Inc. Used under
licence. *Fortune* and Time Inc. are not affiliated with, and do not endorse
products or services of Oxford University Press; p.45 and 49 from *Marketing*
by Baines, Fill & Paige (2010) 1375 words from pp.229–231, 435–438. By
permission of Oxford University Press; p.53 Extract from 'America's century
is over, but it will fight on' by Larry Elliot, *The Guardian,* 23 August 2010.
Copyright Guardian News & Media Ltd 2010. Reproduced by permission;
p.57 Extracts from 'What we can all learn from Amazon about seeing
business opportunities others don't see' by Glenn Llopis, 7 February 2011
from Forbes.com. Reprinted by permission of Forbes Media LLC © 2011; p.61
From *Management and Organisational Behaviour 8E* by Laurie Mullins, Pearson
Education Ltd. © Laurie J. Mullins, 1985, 1989, 1993, 1996, 1999, 2002, 2005,
2007. Chapters 4, 6 © Linda Carter and Laurie J. Mullins 1993, 1996, 1999,
2002, 2005, 2007. Chapter 5 © Linda Carter 1993, 1996, 1999, 2002, 2005,
2007. Chapter 17 © David Preece 1999, 2002, 2005. Reproduced by permission;
p.65 'E&Y CEO on what makes global leaders successful' by James S. Turley, 23
January 2011 from Davos Journal 2011. Reproduced by permission of Ernst &
Young © 2011 EYGM Limited. All Rights Reserved.

Cover photograph by: Gareth Boden Photography

All illustrations by: Rob Briggs Roarr Design

The publishers would like to thank the following for permission to use their photographs:
Alamy Images pp.17 (Stock trader/Simon Belcher), 25 (Chinatown, Singapore/
Robert Harding Picture Library), 56 (Amazon website/Newscast); Corbis
pp.13 (Mother with child/Alix Minde/PhotoAlto), 61 (Business meeting/Laura
Doss/Fancy); Getty Images pp.32 (Business meeting/artparadigm), 53 (Traders/
Daniel Acker/Bloomberg via Getty Images); Masterfile p.65 (Business meeting);
The Advertising Archives p.21 (Cadillac advert, 1958/Image Courtesy of The
Advertising Archives).